Macbeth on the Loose

Robert Walker

For Suzie

Heinemann Educational Publishers
Halley Court, Jordan Hill, Oxford OX2 8EJ
Part of Harcourt Education

Heinemann is the registered trademark of Harcourt Educational Limited

OXFORD MELBOURNE AUCKLAND
JOHANNESBURG BLANTYRE GABORONE
IBADAN PORTSMOUTH (NH)USA CHICAGO

© Robert Walker, 2002

05 04 03
10 9 8 7 6 5 4 3 2

ISBN
0 435 23333 5

Cover design by Miller, Craig and Cocking
Cover illustration by Beccy Blake
Typeset by 🔨 Tek-Art
Printed in the UK by Clays Ltd, St Ives plc

Tel: 01865 888058 www.heinemann.co.uk

Contents

Macbeth on the Loose was first performed at Lytchett Minster Secondary School and Arts College, on 8 December 2000, with the following cast:

Edward	Michael Handley
Alexis	Tania McShane
Gordon	Lee Leonard
Nigel	Kyall Stanley
Timothy	Michael Horn
Sue	Louise Watton
Meg	Jenny Rhodes
Lil	Zoe Harvey
Mr Atherton	Jack Watson
Mrs Painter	Nicola Hann
Roger	Andrew Wellsted
Scott	Joseph Clarke
Lloyd	Daniel Mason
Charlie	Ahmed Qaddoura
Lara	Catherine Leech
Kirsty	Hannah Chivers
Amy	Helen Jeffery
Drew	Vanessa Mulholland
Zara	Emma Knight

The play was directed by Robert Walker.

Introduction

When I was at school, teachers never stopped going on about how fantastic Shakespeare was. In fact they went on about him so much that sometimes I almost got him muddled up with God. In my mind they were, kind of, in the same category.

I remember being so excited when our teacher told us, one day, that we would be studying one of Shakespeare's comedies. If what they said about him was true, surely this would be the mother of all comedies. I imagined myself rolling in the aisles, unable to control the hysteria caused by the genius, the master of mirth.

I didn't laugh once. It wasn't even *nearly* funny. Every so often, as we read, the teacher would laugh, and each time we all looked up in confusion, wondering what little gem we'd just missed. By the end of the play I felt like I had been cheated. I was convinced that anyone claiming to genuinely appreciate this rubbish was either a liar or an idiot.

It wasn't until years later that I decided to go back to Shakespeare's work and have another go. I sat down with a copy of *As You Like It* in one hand, and Brodie's notes in the other, and I told myself I wasn't going to leave the desk until I had read *and* understood it. Gradually, as my determination led me on, what appeared like a play written entirely in riddles slowly became more understandable, until eventually I felt I had truly cracked the code of this seemingly impenetrable language.

The best thing about it was, it was worth all the trouble. For the first time ever I managed to see what my teachers must have seen all those years ago. What I read, and what I continued to read, truly did enrich my whole understanding of life.

Macbeth on the Loose aims to make the ideas and themes within a complex story more accessible and understandable to a younger generation. The parallel story it offers hopefully demonstrates to you how the themes within *Macbeth*, and the message it embodies, are as relevant now as they ever were. It is also intended to be a whole lot of fun, and to take the heaviness out of what is – let's face it – quite a heavy story.

A note for teachers

The play is intended for classroom reading as well as performance. The practical or technical requirements needed to stage the play are few, and the action is deliberately fairly simplistic to set, to make it as accessible as possible.

Should the play be used purely as a classroom reader, to assist with the study of *Macbeth*, I hope the activities I have provided will offer you a variety of ways to explore the text and understand the action. They have also been designed to complement specific objectives within *The Framework for Teaching English for Years 7–9,* and these objectives are highlighted at the start of each task.

Robert Walker

Macbeth on the Loose

Main characters

Edward	(Macbeth)
Alexis	(Lady Macbeth)
Gordon	(Macduff)
Nigel	(Banquo)
Timothy	(Malcolm)

Sue	
Meg	(Tea ladies)
Lil	

Mr Atherton	
Mrs Painter	(Teachers)

Minor characters

Roger	(Porter)
Scott	(Messenger)
Lloyd	(Stand in)
Charlie	(Bully)
Lara	(Servant)

Kirsty	
Amy	(Witches)
Zara	

Drew	(Murderer)

The action of the play centres around Grantham High School where a production of *Macbeth* is in the making.

As a low eerie light comes up, three tea ladies are sitting around a tea-trolley quietly drinking tea. Behind them on the trolley an urn bubbles away like a cauldron. Meg, one of the ladies, is studying the bottom of a cup with great concentration.

SUE   Who is it then?

Pause. The others look on in tremendous anticipation.

MEG   It's difficult to say.

LIL   Go on Meg, have a go!

Pause.

MEG   *(with finality)* Big hands! That's all I can say. He's going to have a couple of whoppers.

SUE   Is that it? Is that all I get after all the years I've known you? You set me up with some freak of nature.

MEG   I don't do no matchmaking, you know that Sue, I just see what I see. It's all in the leaves. The match has already been made.

SUE   Says who! *(She shifts her body away from them, crosses her legs and folds her arms.)* Well, I don't want him. I'm not having him.

LIL   Cheer up love. All it means is he'll have bigger palms to catch your tears, more hand to stroke your brow.

SUE   Probably knock me out.

LIL   Nonsense.

SUE   I said I wanted someone mature, outgoing, with a good sense of humour.

LIL   I'm sure he's got a good sense of humour . . . he'd have to have really.

MEG	I can have another look if you like.
SUE	No, forget it. I think I'll stick with me husband.
MEG	*(contemplating)* Oh. Alas. Once more like fools they rush in . . .
SUE	Shut up! Please!
LIL	Not now Meg.
MEG	*(launching into her speech like a prophet of old)* This generation are all too desperate to know what's around the corner for them. Horoscopes. Crystal balls. Mystics giving them their fortune. And they always assume the future's bright. They build their home in the land of milk and honey long before the chickens have hatched.
SUE	What's she on about?
LIL	I don't know.
MEG	*(looking up)* Why was I chosen! Wherefore is the reason?
LIL	Meg!
MEG	Spare me these visions!
SUE	Spare us all.
MEG	Relinquish them!
SUE AND LIL	*(in unison)* Meg!

Meg stops and looks at them. Her trance is broken.

SUE	You're a tea lady! You work in Grantham High School! You read tea leaves and you're *never* right! They *never* come true!
MEG	Don't they?
LIL	Well, not so far love.
MEG	*(to Sue)* Well, what are *you* worrying about then?
SUE	'Cause one day they might.

MEG   *(hopefully)* One day.

SUE   And who knows what poor fool's gonna get stung.

Pause.

LIL   Cuppa tea?

MEG   Maybe just one more.

They laugh. Lights fade.

Lights up on Edward, a short but quite robust-looking boy, about fourteen. He is standing on a chair trying to recite some lines from Macbeth. *His mate Nigel is watching from the floor.*

NIGEL   Are you ready?

EDWARD   *(bracing himself)* What bit shall I read?

NIGEL   Any bit Macbeth says.

Pause. Edward finds a bit.

EDWARD   *(reading)* Wherefore did you so?

NIGEL   *(searching his script)* Where does he say that?

EDWARD   At the bottom.

NIGEL   That's Macduff!

EDWARD   Who's he?

NIGEL   Well, I don't know, but he's not *Macbeth* is he? You said you wanted to read Macbeth.

EDWARD   Alright! It's confusing. You didn't say there was two Macs. Did I sound quite good anyway?

NIGEL   It sounded like you didn't know what the line meant.

EDWARD   I don't.

NIGEL   You can't act a line if you don't know what it means.

EDWARD   No one knows what Shakespeare means, you just gotta make out like you do.

NIGEL   Well you didn't do it very well.

EDWARD   You told me I was a brilliant actor!

NIGEL   You are.

EDWARD   I only came to this stupid audition to keep you company.

NIGEL	You came 'cause I told you there'd be lots of girls here.
EDWARD	Yeah, and where are they?
NIGEL	We're still early.

Pause. Edward looks at his watch.

EDWARD	Who's gonna be here?
NIGEL	*Amy Hart.*

Pause. Nigel waits for a response.

EDWARD	Is that supposed to impress me?
NIGEL	She's lovely.
EDWARD	She smells of goats, everyone knows that. Her mum lets them live in the house.
NIGEL	Rubbish.
EDWARD	Who else?
NIGEL	Lara Tomlin.

Edward throws his hands in the air in despair.

EDWARD	Oh super! Forget Shakespeare, one more and we can do *the three little pigs.*
NIGEL	What's wrong with Lara?
EDWARD	Who else?
NIGEL	Zara Lord.

Edward looks even more stunned.

What?

EDWARD	Someone else . . . quickly . . . before I leave.
NIGEL	*(dismissive)* I hear Alexis might come.

Edward's face suddenly lifts.

EDWARD	How could you not mention that?

NIGEL	I don't know what you see in her, I think she's horrible.
EDWARD	What are you talking about? The girl is sent from heaven. She's an angel.
NIGEL	Not from what I hear.
EDWARD	Thank you, God. Thank you. *(He goes to his coat and takes out a bottle of aftershave. He puts some on.)* This calls for some serious preparation.
NIGEL	What are you doing?
EDWARD	What do you think? If you wanna catch the fish, you gotta bait the hook.
NIGEL	*(to himself)* If you wanna catch the fish, probably best not intoxicate it at twenty feet.
EDWARD	Now all I need is a lucky charm. *(He proudly takes out from his jacket pocket what looks like a pack of playing cards.)*
NIGEL	What are they?
EDWARD	*(proudly) Nude* playing cards.

Nigel doesn' t look impressed.

	Well, topless.
NIGEL	Why have you got those?
EDWARD	I won them.
NIGEL	Where?
EDWARD	At a fair. Wanna see?
NIGEL	No.
EDWARD	What do you mean?
NIGEL	No, I don't wanna see.

Pause.

EDWARD	*(surprised)* Why not?

NIGEL   I think it's degrading.

Pause. Edward is still surprised.

EDWARD   Why on earth do I go round with you?

Pause.

NIGEL   'Cause I'm your best mate.

Pause. Edward smiles.

EDWARD   Yeah, you are. *(He looks back to his cards.)* Now
which one of you beauties is going to be today's
lucky charm? *(He closes his eyes and plucks a card
from the pack.)* The winner is . . . *(opens eyes)* Gloria!
Looking quite glorious if I may say so. *(He puts the
card in his shirt pocket, symbolically by his heart.)* You,
my darling, get to stay right by my heart. You must
bring me luck today, you hear?

NIGEL   Do you normally talk to them?

EDWARD   Sometimes.

Nigel shakes his head.

It works! They bring me luck. I want the lead role.

NIGEL   Since when?

EDWARD   Since I have a young lady to impress. *(He notices
something and goes to an imaginary window.)* Nigel,
you did say the audition was here, didn't you?

NIGEL   No, *you* did. Why?

EDWARD   'Cause the lights are on in the hall and there's lots
of people standing round looking like they're at
an audition.

Nigel runs to the window.

NIGEL   They are! You got the wrong room, idiot!

They run out.

We've probably missed it!

EDWARD   I'm sorry. Can't remember everything.

As the lights come up, bright and strong, we see a large school hall with people in small groups standing around talking excitedly, papers in their hands. A young woman, Mrs Painter, calls them together.

MRS PAINTER Okay! Everyone on stage in a line!

Everyone immediately runs to the stage and bustles to get the centre position.

Don't push! Everyone will get their moment of stardom.

Gordon, a zealous young cadet, wearing his badge and an official-looking blue beret, suddenly hauls a kid out of the line by the back of his collar. The kid shrieks.

GORDON End of the line!

MRS PAINTER Gordon, what's the problem?

GORDON Johnson, Miss. He was behaving in an inappropriate and foolish manner.

MRS PAINTER I see.

GORDON It's been dealt with.

MRS PAINTER So I see. In future, Gordon, if you could leave the punishment of subordinates to me, I'd appreciate it.

GORDON As you wish, Ma'am.

MRS PAINTER Now, does everyone have their audition lines? Let me see them.

The cast hold their papers up.

Good.

ROGER Why have we only got a couple of lines each?

MRS PAINTER	Because that is all someone like myself needs in order to see your potential, what you are truly capable of.
ROGER	Oh.
MRS PAINTER	Understand?
ROGER	Alright.

Pause.

MRS PAINTER	Right . . . *team*, so this is what I've got, is it? You lot are the clay from which I am to mould a classic piece of Shakespearean theatre. *Macbeth*!

Pause. There is stillness among the group.

ALEXIS	I'm very good.
EDWARD	So am I.
MRS PAINTER	Excellent, well, we shall see.
NIGEL	He is, Miss, Edward's brilliant.
MRS PAINTER	I'm sure he is, Nigel. I'm sure many of you are very talented. Now, first things first, starting from Roger, I'd like each of you, in turn, to step forward, tell me your full name and what part you would like to be considered for. Go.
ROGER	Roger Johnson. Macbeth.
TIMOTHY	Timothy Evans. Macbeth.
SCOTT	Scott Norton. Macbeth.
LLOYD	Lloyd Stevens . . . Macbeth.
MRS PAINTER	I can see a pattern emerging here.
EDWARD	Edward Owen. Macbeth.
ALEXIS	Alexis Dupont. Juliet.
MRS PAINTER	Wrong play, Alexis.
ALEXIS	Really?

MRS PAINTER	Yep.
ALEXIS	Are you sure?
MRS PAINTER	Oh yes.
ALEXIS	*(disappointed)* Oh.
MRS PAINTER	Would you like to be a witch?
ALEXIS	No I wouldn't! Is there anyone a little bit like Juliet?
NIGEL	What about Lady Macbeth? She sounds quite nice.
ALEXIS	Yes! *Lady* Macbeth! Put me down for her.
MRS PAINTER	Right you are. Carry on.
NIGEL	Nigel Cummings. I don't mind who I play.
MRS PAINTER	Thank you, Nigel.
GORDON	Gordon Burbidge. Macduff.
MRS PAINTER	Oh, that's interesting. A break from the pack. Gordon, what provoked this very original preference?
GORDON	Well, Miss, I've read the play and it seems that Macduff is the real hero.
EDWARD	*(contradicting)* Macbeth's got *miles* more lines.
MRS PAINTER	Shhh! Carry on Gordon.
GORDON	And, well, it seems he's the most righteous, which is important 'cause I can't stand unlawfulness, corruption, makes me sick. That's why I'm Lance Corporal, in my detachment.
MRS PAINTER	Detachment?
GORDON	Cadets, Miss.
	A couple of the boys do mock salutes, then snigger.
EDWARD	That's why he wears his hat.
SCOTT	All the time.
LLOYD	Never takes it off.

ROGER	None of the other cadets wear their hats.
GORDON	*(defensively)* So!
ALEXIS	It's not the *real* army anyway.
GORDON	I am a real soldier!
ALEXIS	You lot are little boys. You run around with maps and plastic guns pretending there's a war.
GORDON	I have honour and fortitude.
EDWARD	And a plastic gun.

The others laugh.

GORDON	They are not plastic. *Scoff* all you like! You could rely on me in the battlefield.
MRS PAINTER	I think that's brilliant, Gordon.
GORDON	Thank you, Miss.

Suddenly various members of the line, in turn, jolt forward, wincing with pain, as someone passes behind them. Roger is tripped up and falls forward, Timothy screams, as his hair is pulled, and Alexis leaps forward with a shriek, as if her bottom has just been pinched. From behind the line, a tall tough-looking kid emerges, Charlie Slater. He smiles at them all with an insane grin.

MRS PAINTER	What's going on? How can we help you, Mr Slater?
CHARLIE	Fear not, countrymen! Charlie's here, and he's ready to act!

The cast groan.

Get over it, I'm here to stay.

GORDON	Think again.

On seeing Gordon, Charlie sighs with disappointment.

CHARLIE	Oh no.

MRS PAINTER	Do you wish to audition, Charlie?
GORDON	No, he doesn't. *(Gordon goes to the door and motions for Charlie to leave.)* Come on! On your way!
MRS PAINTER	Gordon, what on earth is going on? This boy is perfectly entitled to audition. It's open to everyone.
GORDON	Not to this bad apple. Charlie is prohibited from involvement with any and all extra-curricular activities. He's been found guilty of bullying throughout the school. I'm sorry, Miss.

Pause.

| MRS PAINTER | I see. On your way, Charlie. |

Charlie walks out, staring at Gordon.

| CHARLIE | *(to Gordon)* One day, I'm gonna . . . |
| GORDON | Be careful. If you threaten me, I *will* engage. |

Charlie goes.

MRS PAINTER	Right, back to work. Who's left?
LARA	Lara Tomlin. Don't mind.
KIRSTY	Kirsty Moores.
AMY	Amy Hart.
DREW	Drew Mitchel.
ZARA	Zara Lord. We all want to be witches.
MRS PAINTER	Trouble is, there's only three. I'll see what I can do.
DREW	Can I wear a false beard?
MRS PAINTER	*(confused)* Umm . . . possibly.
DREW	Thank you.
MRS PAINTER	Right, now, *Macbeth*.

Everyone in the line gears themselves up ready for action.

Has anyone, apart from Gordon, read *Macbeth*?

No response.

Does anyone have any idea what it's about?

Pause. They deflate a little.

TIMOTHY   Scotland?

Pause. No more responses.

MRS PAINTER   Okay. Good. Right. Where shall we start? I think the best idea is if I give you a basic outline of the first Act and then at least you'll know whereabouts the bit you're reading fits in. Okay?

ALL   Yeah.

MRS PAINTER   Now, to start with there's this king. Edward, step forward, I'd like you to play the King.

EDWARD   Excellent!

MRS PAINTER   The King is not Macbeth.

EDWARD   *(disappointed)* Oh.

MRS PAINTER   Let's have you far right please.

Edward moves to that position.

MRS PAINTER   Now, on the far left there's a battle going on and Macbeth and Banquo are in the thick of it, fighting on the King's behalf. Timothy, if you'd like to play Macbeth.

The other contenders groan.

Just for the time being and, Nigel, if you'd like to play Banquo. Far left please, boys.

They go.

And you're fighting.

Timothy suddenly punches Nigel on the arm quite hard.

NIGEL   Ahh!

MRS PAINTER   Not each other, idiots!

NIGEL   I didn't do anything!

MRS PAINTER   You're fighting the King's enemies!

NIGEL   *(to Timothy)* Idiot.

TIMOTHY   *(to Mrs Painter)* Sorry.

MRS PAINTER   Start fighting then.

NIGEL   *(looking around)* Where are they?

MRS PAINTER   Just imagine they're there.

NIGEL   Righto.

They start fist-fighting an imaginary enemy.

MRS PAINTER   Use your swords!

They change to swords.

Good, that's better. Now, one of the less important soldiers who's also at the battle, um . . . Scott. *(She motions for him to join Nigel and Timothy.)*

SCOTT   *(disappointed)* Oh, cheers.

MRS PAINTER   Travels back to the King over hill and dale, to tell him how the battle is looking. *(to Scott)* Start travelling then.

Scott slowly crosses the stage from left to right pretending he's on a horse.

When he gets to the King he tells him all about how well Macbeth is doing.

She waits. Scott twigs.

SCOTT   *(stilted)* Macbeth's doing really well.

MRS PAINTER	And the King is delighted.
	Pause. She waits.
EDWARD	That's super.
MRS PAINTER	Now, the King decides he is so delighted with Macbeth, he's going to award him the title 'Thane of Cawdor'. So how do you feel about that, Macbeth?
TIMOTHY	*(confused)* Well, alright, I suppose.
MRS PAINTER	Do you know what that means?
TIMOTHY	Not exactly.
MRS PAINTER	Gordon?
GORDON	A thane is a man who's given land by the king or other superior for outstanding military service.
TIMOTHY	That's nice.
MRS PAINTER	Exactly. So the King sends some people off to tell Macbeth the good news. Scott, you're now the other messenger. Start travelling . . .

Scott starts going back in the other direction on his horse.

And freeze!

Scott freezes at the start of his journey.

Now, about this time, Macbeth and Banquo finish their battle and are victorious.

Nigel and Timothy hold their swords up and cheer.

And they start their journey back to the King.

They start travelling.

And freeze!

They freeze.

Now something very spooky happens.

Mrs Painter looks afraid. The cast look round at each other.

TIMOTHY   What?

MRS PAINTER   On their journey back to the King and before the King's messenger gets to them, they are met on the path by three strange figures. These are the three witches. Well, at present there's four. Come on girls!

The girls come to the middle.

LLOYD   Are they real witches?

MRS PAINTER   Oh yes.

LARA   Are they evil?

MRS PAINTER   Very.

DREW   Can I wear a false beard?

MRS PAINTER   Possibly, I said, possibly. Now when Macbeth and Banquo meet these strange-looking figures on the path, what do you think must be going through their minds? Let's see the meeting. Go.

The boys step into character.

TIMOTHY   Look ahead, Banquo. Who are those strange-looking strumpets on our path?

MRS PAINTER   Good, Tim.

NIGEL   I don't know, Macbeth, but they don't look very nice.

AMY   'Ello, 'ello, boys. Mind if we have a little word in your ear?

MRS PAINTER   You're not a policeman, Amy. Try it more like a witch might speak.

AMY	Macbeth! Banquo!
NIGEL	How do you know our names?
MRS PAINTER	Good response, Nigel. Now, at this point the witches tell them what? Gordon?
GORDON	That Macbeth is going to be given the title 'Thane of Cawdor' and that later he'll be King.
LLOYD	How do the witches know that the King's gonna make him a thane?
AMY	'Cause they're magic, dummy.
ROGER	Are they lying about him becoming King?
MRS PAINTER	Yes and no.
ROGER	Eh?
MRS PAINTER	All will become clear, Roger. Now, Macbeth, do you think you believe them?
TIMOTHY	No.
MRS PAINTER	Improvise it. Let's see what their response might be. Go!
AMY	Macbeth! Banquo!
NIGEL	How do you know our names?
DREW	Never you mind.
ZARA	Secrets we have for you. Fortunes to bestow.
MRS PAINTER	Good, Zara! Good word.
TIMOTHY	Not tonight thanks girls, I'm washing me hair.
NIGEL	You're just some dirty old hags. What could you possibly have to interest us?
MRS PAINTER	Good!
AMY	Visions of a bright future if you'll hear.
TIMOTHY	Oh, go on then.
DREW	You, Macbeth, are going to become 'Thane of Cawdor' and later . . .

ZARA	King!

The boys start laughing.

TIMOTHY	Yeah, right!
NIGEL	*(sarcastically)* Allow me, your Highness, to kiss your feet. *(He mimes kissing feet.)*
MRS PAINTER	Then suddenly they vanish! Just like that!

The girls go back to the line.

How do you feel now?

TIMOTHY	Slightly spooked.
MRS PAINTER	A little less dismissive?
NIGEL	Yeah.
MRS PAINTER	Imagine how much more unsettled you feel, then, when the messenger arrives and tells you it's true, you *are* Thane of Cawdor.

She drags Scott over and throws him in front of them. He looks annoyed.

SCOTT	The King has sent me to tell you that you are now Thane of Cawdor.
TIMOTHY	I'm thinking . . . gosh!
MRS PAINTER	I bet you are.
NIGEL	He's thinking, if the witches are right about that, perhaps that means I will be King.
MRS PAINTER	You carry on, on your journey . . .

They continue.

And, all the time, what are you thinking . . . ?

TIMOTHY	I'm gonna be King! I am gonna be King!
MRS PAINTER	Gordon. Whisper to Edward what the King tells Macbeth when he reaches him. Carry on riding, boys.

The boys carry on their ride towards the King. Gordon whispers to Edward what he must say on their arrival. Eventually they arrive.

EDWARD Greetings, noble friends!

MRS PAINTER Super voice, Edward! Well done!

EDWARD Put down your swords and rest your weary feet.

NIGEL Thank you.

TIMOTHY Thank you.

EDWARD Thank *you*, worthy Thane, you received my message?

TIMOTHY Yeah, cheers for that.

EDWARD I can at this point also disclose who I have in mind as my successor to the throne.

MRS PAINTER Lovely language, Edward. Well done!

Nigel and Timothy's faces lift in anticipation.

EDWARD My son! Malcolm!

Mrs Painter points to Lloyd. Lloyd steps forward.

TIMOTHY You're joking!

NIGEL But the witches said . . .

MRS PAINTER That's right. How does Macbeth feel?

TIMOTHY Those stupid witches!

MRS PAINTER Good!

TIMOTHY Getting my hopes up like that! I wanna be King!

MRS PAINTER What do you think you're going to do now?

TIMOTHY Cry?

MRS PAINTER No.

TIMOTHY I don't know.

MRS PAINTER You're going to go back to your wife and tell her the bad news.

TIMOTHY	Who's my wife?
MRS PAINTER	Lady Macbeth.
TIMOTHY	She doesn't know the *good* news yet.
MRS PAINTER	Yes she does.
TIMOTHY	How?
MRS PAINTER	You wrote her a letter.
TIMOTHY	Did I? When did I do that?
MRS PAINTER	You sent a messenger after you'd seen the witches and been told you were the Thane. She thinks you're going to be the King. Now Alexis . . .

Alexis springs forward, ready for action.

ALEXIS	Yes!
MRS PAINTER	You are Lady Macbeth, and you are crazy about your husband.

Alexis observes Timothy with a look of slight disgust.

ALEXIS	I don't have to kiss him, do I?
MRS PAINTER	Timothy hasn't got the part yet.
ALEXIS	Yeah, but if he does, I'm not kissing him. I think she's a bit out of his league.
TIMOTHY	Don't flatter yourself, Alexis.
ALEXIS	I think underneath it all she's got a bit of a thing for the King.

Alexis gives Edward a seductive look. Edward blushes.

MRS PAINTER	No, I think you've got that all wrong. She's crazy about Macbeth but she thinks he's a bit weak. And she wants to be Queen even more than Macbeth wants to be King. She'll do anything to be Queen.
ALEXIS	What do I do?
MRS PAINTER	You persuade Macbeth to kill the King.

ALEXIS	I do not!
MRS PAINTER	I'm afraid you do.
ALEXIS	I wouldn't do that! I'm a lady!
MRS PAINTER	You deliberately make him feel like he's not a man unless he does it.
ALEXIS	Ladies don't manipulate men like that.
MRS PAINTER	Well, this one does.

Pause. Alexis looks annoyed.

ALEXIS	It just shows you how out of date this story is.
MRS PAINTER	No, it isn't. Don't be so insolent.
ALEXIS	It was written like . . . a million years ago.
MRS PAINTER	Four hundred, actually.
ALEXIS	Exactly!
MRS PAINTER	*(annoyed)* What do you mean?
ALEXIS	Well, things have changed . . . Y'know, computers, cars . . .
LLOYD	Aeroplanes.
SCOTT	Forklift trucks.
MRS PAINTER	Yes, I realise *things* have changed . . .
ROGER	Sliced bread.
MRS PAINTER	Oh, shut up!

They are quiet.

I realise *things* have changed, but *people* haven't.
See? Put up your hand if you see what I mean.

No one raises their hand.

I see. Well, hopefully when we've done the play,
you will.

Now! Where were we? Yes, I think that's it! The first
Act finishes with the King telling Macbeth he wants
to come to his house for dinner and a sleep-over.

ALEXIS	That's a bit forward, isn't it?
MRS PAINTER	It's the *King*. Right then! In a line!

They all run to the stage.

	If you're a star, this is your chance to shine.

The line is formed.

	In turn, step forward, say the character I've given you, where the bit comes and then give me the lines.
LLOYD	You've only given me one line to say.
MRS PAINTER	It's quality, not quantity, Lloyd. Okay everyone?
ALL	Yes.

Pause.

MRS PAINTER	Right. Go!
ROGER	This is the King when he first sees the messenger come from the battle to say how they're doing. 'What bloody man is that? He can report, As seemeth by his plight, of the revolt The newest state.'
MRS PAINTER	Good.
TIMOTHY	Macbeth when the witches have told him the news. 'Stay, you imperfect speakers, tell me more. By Sinel's death, I know I am Thane of Glamis,'
SCOTT	I carry it on. 'But how of Cawdor? The Thane of Cawdor lives A prosperous gentleman; and to be king Stands not within the prospect of belief,'
LLOYD	*(despondent)* 'No more than to be Cawdor.'
MRS PAINTER	Come on Lloyd, make the most of it!
LLOYD	*(louder)* 'No more than to be Cawdor!'

MRS PAINTER	Not necessarily louder, my sweet. Perhaps with more intensity.
LLOYD	*(low gruff voice)* 'No more than to be Cawdor.'
AMY	He sounds like one of the witches.
MRS PAINTER	No he doesn't, that was good, Lloyd. Alexis?
ALEXIS	Lady Macbeth, before Macbeth arrives. 'Come you spirits That tend on mortal thoughts, *unsex me here,* And fill me from the crown to the toe top-full Of direst cruelty;'
MRS PAINTER	I'm sure that's not the bit I gave you, was it, Alexis?
ALEXIS	Well, no, but I preferred this bit, it's a bit more *risqué*.
MRS PAINTER	I see. Amy?
AMY	We've already got a bit prepared. We did it last night. Can we show you that?
MRS PAINTER	Yes, by all means.

The four girls, Amy, Drew, Kirsty, Zara, come forward in a line. Amy runs to the wings and produces a tape recorder, she presses play and returns to the line. A backing beat comes on and in time with the beat they begin a dance. It looks like a girl-band routine.

ALL	Double, double toil and trouble; Fire burn, and cauldron bubble.
AMY	Fillet of a fenny snake,
KIRSTY	In the cauldron boil and bake;
DREW	Eye of newt, and toe of frog,
ZARA	Wool of bat, and tongue of dog,
ALL	Adder's fork, and blind-worm's sting, Lizard's leg, and howlet's wing, For a charm of powerful trouble,

AMY	Like a hell-broth boil and bubble!
ALL	Double, double toil and trouble; Fire burn, and cauldron bubble.

They finish with a leap in the air. The class applaud, except Edward and Alexis.

MRS PAINTER	Well done girls, very imaginative. Right, Edward?
EDWARD	*(excited)* Yes!
MRS PAINTER	Your turn!

Pause. Edward prepares himself. He is just about to come out with the first line, when suddenly there is a loud noise as the tea-trolley crashes through the doors, into the hall.

MEG	Tea time everyone!
MRS PAINTER	Oh, excellent.

All rush to the trolley apart from Edward, Nigel, Lara and Gordon.

EDWARD	Wait, hang on a minute! Some of us haven't read yet!
NIGEL	I haven't read yet either, Miss.
MRS PAINTER	No I know, nor have Lara or Gordon. Don't worry about it, I've seen enough. It doesn't take *me* long to know. I'll put the cast list on the noticeboard tomorrow. Don't forget to look.
NIGEL	Can't you tell us now?
MRS PAINTER	No! It wouldn't be proper.
NIGEL	I bet you've given me a rubbish part.
MRS PAINTER	Why on earth would you say that?
NIGEL	'Cause I'm not very good.
MRS PAINTER	I think you're lovely. *(She smiles.)*

NIGEL	Thank you.

She goes. All except Edward and Nigel go to the trolley. Edward looks extremely disgruntled.

EDWARD	That's not fair!
NIGEL	It'll be alright.
GORDON	*(trying to get the queue in some sort of order)* One at a time please!
ALEXIS	I was first! Thank you.
EDWARD	*(sulking)* That's not fair!
NIGEL	You were very good in there.
EDWARD	She didn't let me read Macbeth.
NIGEL	Maybe she didn't need to.
EDWARD	Tim was rubbish.
NIGEL	He was alright.
EDWARD	Nigel, he couldn't even fight properly.
NIGEL	What do you mean?
EDWARD	He was using his sword like it was one of those . . . feather dusters.
NIGEL	Was he?
EDWARD	Oh yeah.
NIGEL	I was too busy fighting myself. Did you see me? . . . Ed?

Edward notices Alexis staring at him from across the room. He looks hypnotised. She is holding two teacups and motions for him to take one of them. She slowly moves towards him. He timidly goes to meet her in the centre.

ALEXIS	Hello.

Pause.

EDWARD	Hello.
ALEXIS	You were very good.
EDWARD	Thank you.
ALEXIS	Better than all the other boys.
EDWARD	Thank you.

Pause.

ALEXIS	I got you a tea.

She hands him the cup.

EDWARD	*(nervous)* Thank you.
ALEXIS	You do like tea?
EDWARD	Oh yes.
ALEXIS	I knew it. All the *children* are having orange squash. The tea is for the adults. I had a feeling that me and you probably . . . *drank from the same cup* . . . know what I mean?

Edward nods slowly, still hypnotised. Nigel, who has been earwigging on the conversation, looks irritated. He pipes up.

NIGEL	I drink tea too, Miss *Mature*.
EDWARD	*(appeasing)* Ignore him. *(He turns to Nigel.)* Shut up Nigel. *(He turns back and is instantly mesmerised again.)*
ALEXIS	I've got a feeling you and me are going to be the King and Queen of this show. It's like a premonition.
EDWARD	Really?
ALEXIS	*(nodding)* Would you like that?

Edward nods slowly.

Let's drink on it, cheers.

They slowly touch cups, staring into each other's eyes, and drink.

Can I ask you something personal? Something . . . quite . . . *naughty*?

Edward excitedly nods his head. Suddenly she notices something in his shirt pocket.

Why are there two big bosoms sticking out of your shirt pocket?

EDWARD What?

ALEXIS There's a lady coming out of your shirt pocket.

Edward's heart stops. He looks down to see Gloria coming out of her hiding place.

EDWARD Oh no.

ALEXIS What is it, Edward? Who is she?

NIGEL *(shouting)* It's Gloria.

ALEXIS Who's Gloria?

Edward takes the card out of his shirt pocket.

EDWARD *(anxiously)* It's just a playing card, look. *(He shows it to her. He then gets the pack out.)* Look, there's a whole pack. They're just playing cards, that's all.

Pause.

ALEXIS I think that's degrading.

EDWARD So do I!

ALEXIS What do you mean?

EDWARD I do as well.

ALEXIS Well, why have you got them then?

EDWARD	I haven't.
ALEXIS	You have.
EDWARD	I haven't.
ALEXIS	What do you mean?
EDWARD	They're not mine.
ALEXIS	Whose are they?

Pause. Edward points at Nigel.

EDWARD	Nigel's.
NIGEL	What!
EDWARD	We play cards. It was the only pack we could find. He won them at a fair. Didn't you? . . . Nigel?
ALEXIS	Did you, Nigel?

Edward mimes 'Please' with his lips. Nigel finally caves in.

NIGEL	*(grudgingly)* That's right.
ALEXIS	That's alright then.

Edward forces the cards into Nigel's possession.

ALEXIS	*(to Edward)* I'll see *you* after. You can walk me home.

She leaves with an affectionate little wave, he returns it. Nigel takes her place.

NIGEL	How could you do that?
EDWARD	*(grovelling)* I'm sorry.
NIGEL	I can't believe you.
EDWARD	I didn't have a choice.
NIGEL	You could have told the truth!
EDWARD	I would have lost her! I would have lost my chance with her!

NIGEL	You can have these back!

He tries to hand Edward the cards.

EDWARD	I can't!
NIGEL	*I* don't want them!
EDWARD	I'm walking her home, you heard, she might find them!
NIGEL	Hide them!
EDWARD	I *hid* Gloria. *(pause)* Look, just look after them for me, just for a bit.
NIGEL	Where would I put them?
EDWARD	Under your mattress.
NIGEL	You know what my mum's like, if she finds them I've had it.
EDWARD	She's not going to.
NIGEL	You don't appreciate me.
EDWARD	I do! Thank you. Thank you, Nigel.

Meg, the tea lady, comes between them with the trolley.

MEG	Hurry up boys, I need the cups.

The boys drink and hand their cups to her. Meg looks into Nigel's cup.

MEG	Oww . . .
NIGEL	*(confused)* What?
MEG	You're going to do well.

She shows him the tea leaves.

NIGEL	Is that a crystal ball?
MEG	That it is.
NIGEL	What does it say?

MEG	It says you're going to do very well in this here audition, and be given a character to play beginning with B.
NIGEL	B for Banquo. Not a bad part.

Meg looks into Edward's cup.

MEG	Oww . . . And behold it's Macbeth standing before me. Destined to play Macbeth. This will lead you, my son, to even greater things.
NIGEL	Always come out on top, don't you Ed? Always the winner.
MEG	Even greater things.

Nigel turns and walks away. Edward follows.

EDWARD	*(to Nigel)* You don't honestly believe that rubbish.
NIGEL	It's probably true, can't imagine you not getting what you want.
EDWARD	She's not a proper fortune teller.
MEG	*(offended)* These are just my day clothes.
EDWARD	She's just a tea lady, she wipes up other people's mess.
NIGEL	Bit like me really.
EDWARD	No!
MEG	I know what I am talking about!
EDWARD	If you're all knowing, then tell me what I got for Christmas. Listen to this, Nigel.
MEG	*(looking into the cup)* Mummy bought you . . . a bike.
EDWARD	Lucky guess.
MEG	Very expensive . . . yet second-hand.

Edward suddenly looks slightly less smug.

EDWARD	So.
MEG	Looks the business on the outside. Lovely chrome handlebars.

Edward gulps.

Gold-rimmed wheels.

EDWARD	How did you know that?

Mrs Painter pops her head in.

MRS PAINTER	Nigel, can I have a quick word?

Nigel goes, leaving Edward alone with Meg.

MEG	I bet all the boys envy you. Pity they don't know the rest.
EDWARD	What do you mean?
MEG	You know. The gears don't work proper. The back brakes don't engage. The chain slips every time you go up a hill, and let's face it, she doesn't exactly corner like a real babe, does she? Your new bike turned out to be a right disaster. Didn't it?
EDWARD	*(stunned)* How did you know all that?

Nigel comes rushing back in.

NIGEL	I got Banquo! Mrs Painter just told me!
EDWARD	Why did she just tell *you*?
NIGEL	'Cause I'm lovely. I'm not supposed to tell anyone, or they'll all want to know.

Edward is still hypnotised by Meg's stare.

MEG	B . . . B . . . B . . . Banquo.

Edward suddenly realises the implication, and runs off.

EDWARD	I don't believe it! I'm gonna be the star!

Sue and Lil approach Meg with suspicion. Meg is clearing some left-over cups.

SUE   How did you know all that?

LIL   How did you know his Mum bought him a bike?

MEG   *(pausing)* I sold it to her.

They stare at her.

It was our Kevin's. We thought we better get rid of it before he killed himself. Absolute death trap, that bike.

They laugh and slowly walk off stage with the trolley.

LIL   Meg, you are awful.

MEG   Well, he deserved it.

SUE   Hey, you got that other one right.

MEG   Yeah, that was a bit of luck eh?

> *Edward and Alexis are together in a park. Alexis is
> stomping back and forth across the stage, furious, while
> Edward sits, staring at her. He looks stunned.*

EDWARD You must have got it wrong. You must have read
it wrong.

ALEXIS I am an 'A' student. I don't read things *wrong*.

EDWARD Where was it?

ALEXIS *On* the noticeboard, like Mrs Painter said it
would be.

EDWARD Who am I again?

ALEXIS Malcolm!

EDWARD But yesterday . . . the tea lady . . . she said . . .
it was supposed to be me. *I* was supposed to
be . . . Macbeth.

ALEXIS I know!

EDWARD She saw *even greater* things.

> *Pause.*

ALEXIS Tim is disgusting, I can't kiss *him*.

EDWARD Maybe you won't have to.

ALEXIS I *want* to kiss someone, dummy.

EDWARD Do you?

ALEXIS Of course, I'm brilliant at it. *(contemplates)* I want
a proper Macbeth to pull me into him and I'd
be totally in control yet appropriately submissive
as well.

EDWARD *(nervously)* I could kiss you, right now.

ALEXIS Oh yeah, that'll do, I'll ask *Malcolm* to kiss me!

EDWARD Malcolm's not a bad part. I think he's the King's son.

ALEXIS	And what does he do when the King's murdered?
EDWARD	What?
ALEXIS	Runs away. Gordon told me. The man's a wimp!
EDWARD	Yeah, but I'll play him real butch.
ALEXIS	How do you flee from danger in a *butch* way? Tell me! How do you do that!
EDWARD	I don't know, I haven't practised it yet.
ALEXIS	It just doesn't work with *Malcolm*. Listen, does this sound right to you? *(She puts on a deep and husky voice.)* Go forth into battle . . . *Malcolm*. Hold me to your chest and swear your love . . . *Malcolm*. *(shouts)* Malcolm sounds like a middle-aged man who still lives with his mother! I don't want a Malcolm! I want a Macbeth!
EDWARD	*(whispers)* Alright, don't shout. This park's got a warden you know, he kicks you out if you're naughty.
ALEXIS	*(holding her head in her hands)* I can't believe I'm rooting for a man who gets nervous about the park warden.
EDWARD	Well, what can *I* do?
ALEXIS	Do something about it. What kind of man are you? Sitting there meek and mild saying, 'I don't mind being Malcolm, he's okay.' You said yourself it was an unfair audition. She was *unfair*.
EDWARD	So.
ALEXIS	So we get unfair as well. An eye for an eye.
EDWARD	What can we do?
ALEXIS	Well, we agree she doesn't realise your true potential.
EDWARD	Yeah.

ALEXIS	So we get rid of her, and hopefully whoever takes over will.
EDWARD	Get rid of her! You're insane!
ALEXIS	And you're a true Malcolm. I was wrong. That part suits you down to the ground.
EDWARD	Do you mind telling me how exactly you intend to get rid of her?
ALEXIS	We simply find pressing concerns elsewhere which means she is no longer in a position to direct our piece. Easy.
EDWARD	Nasty.
ALEXIS	Come on! Be Macbeth!
EDWARD	I'm trying.
ALEXIS	I mean you're the one whose Mum's a magistrate.
EDWARD	*(confused)* And . . .

Alexis shrugs as if suggesting something obvious.

She can't just get people locked up, y'know!

ALEXIS	She might be able to.
EDWARD	You've gotta be joking.
ALEXIS	She's got to be able to do something! Think about it. Don't let me down. *(She goes.)*

Lights come up on the next rehearsal, the following day. Mrs Painter is nowhere to be seen. The cast are in small groups chattering. Timothy and Nigel are having a pretend sword fight on stage. Alexis and Edward are sitting together, she looks comfortable, he looks anxious. Eventually Nigel kills Timothy with his pretend sword.

NIGEL I got him for you, Ed!

No response.

Eh, do you think she's forgotten us?

No response from Edward.

ALEXIS I'm sure she's just a little held up.

AMY *(pipes up from the witches' group)* She's not usually late.

Suddenly Mr Atherton, the school PE teacher, comes bursting through the doors, in full athletic attire. He blows his whistle, everyone jumps.

MR ATHERTON Okay, people, let's have you on the floor.

No one moves.

Now!

They move. He stands on the stage, pauses until there is silence, and then addresses them.

Right. 'Fraid I've got some bad news for you. You've got me from now on! I am now the director of this show!

ZARA Wha . . . t.

LLOYD No way!

SCOTT	Where's Mrs Painter!
DREW	She can't have pulled out!
MR ATHERTON	Quiet! Apparently Mrs Painter has been unexpectedly asked to do jury service at the local court.
KIRSTY	Why did they ask her to do it?
MR ATHERTON	Everyone gets asked to do it at some point or another. You don't get a choice.
ROGER	That's not fair!
MR ATHERTON	As it could last up to three weeks she's asked me to step in and replace her.
SCOTT	Can you teach drama?
MR ATHERTON	Course I can! I'm a PE teacher! I read the play last night, it's a piece of cake.

They look unimpressed.

Anyway, something else. I also received a note under my office door from Mrs Painter. *(He looks at the note but strains to read it.)* Well, apparently from Mrs Painter, she must have been in an awful hurry. *(He reads it.)* 'Dear Mr Atherton, would you be so kind as to tell the group there was a mistake on the cast list . . . yes . . . sterday,' spelt with two S's. 'Tim mustn't play Macbeth, it should be Edward, he's very good. Give Tim, Malcolm.' *(He looks up.)* Is that clear?

TIMOTHY	*(disbelieving)* What!

Edward stares guiltily ahead. He catches Nigel's glance: it is fixed on him with disgust and accusation. Gordon also looks suspicious.

NIGEL	Edward!

MR ATHERTON	Right, shall we make a start then?
	The group make no move.
	Where did Mrs Painter get up to?
	Alexis jumps up.
ALEXIS	*(eagerly)* We just did the first Act, she talked us through it.
MR ATHERTON	Super! Well, shall we start Act Two then? Come on! Move!
	He blows his whistle loudly. People move to their respective places.
	Right, where's Banquo?
	Nigel comes to the stage.
	Fleance?
	Lloyd comes to the stage.
	Right, you two are outside Macbeth's castle, wandering about. The King's had supper with Macbeth and his Mrs, he's had a good time, he's in bed. Macbeth's about to kill him, but you don't know that. Go.
LLOYD	I'm not sure how to play Fleance at this point, Sir. What do you think?
MR ATHERTON	Um . . . I don't really mind, he's not that important.
LLOYD	Oh.
MR ATHERTON	Do it how you want.
LLOYD	Righto.
	They begin the performance.
NIGEL	How goes the night, boy?

LLOYD	The moon is down; I have not heard the clock.
NIGEL	And she goes down at twelve.
LLOYD	I take 't, 'tis later, sir.
MR ATHERTON	And enter Macbeth. Go!
NIGEL	I've got a whole bit yet.
MR ATHERTON	Yeah, well, we're gonna have to cut bits here and there, otherwise it'll go on all night. Give Macbeth his cue, Banquo. Fleance, go away.

Lloyd walks off.

NIGEL	Who's there?

Edward walks on stage, he stands opposite Nigel. They stare. Nigel looks furious.

EDWARD	A friend.
NIGEL	Huh.

Mr Atherton is studying the script.

MR ATHERTON	Now, you two are good mates.
NIGEL	*Were*.
MR ATHERTON	*(correcting)* At this point you, Banquo, have no idea about Macbeth's intentions.
NIGEL	Oh I think I could take a pretty good guess.
MR ATHERTON	How?
NIGEL	I know how much he wanted to be *King*.
MR ATHERTON	Yes, but . . .
NIGEL	I saw how his eyes lit up when that witch promised him, what was it . . . *even greater things*.
MR ATHERTON	Um . . . I'm not sure those were the exact words she used. *(He ruffles through the script.)*
NIGEL	I think they were.

MR ATHERTON	Well anyway, the main thing is with this bit, is you, Banquo, want to talk to Macbeth about what the witches foretold, 'cause you haven't seen him since you were at the King's palace together when the King announced he was giving the throne to someone else. And at that point I think you sensed Macbeth's disappointment.
NIGEL	I never thought he'd go this far.
MR ATHERTON	Take it from line twenty.

Mr Atherton blows his whistle loudly. People wince with displeasure.

NIGEL	I dreamt last night of the three Weird Sisters.
	To you they have showed some truth.
EDWARD	I think not of them.
NIGEL	*(accusingly)* Yeah, right!
MR ATHERTON	You've got to say the lines that are there, man!
NIGEL	I'm sorry.
MR ATHERTON	'Yeah, right' indeed. Very Shakespearean. Right, what next? Macbeth, you agree to talk about it properly sometime, then Banquo, you go.

Nigel goes.

MR ATHERTON	Now there's a bit here where you see a dagger hovering in mid-air and you wonder what it's all about . . . but we're not gonna do that bit.
GORDON	Isn't that quite an important bit?
MR ATHERTON	It could well be, Gordon, but what I'm interested in is the real *conflict* within the scene, and conflict involves people.
GORDON	But there's a lot of conflict within Macbeth himself during that bit. He's wondering whether it's a stop or go sign.

MR ATHERTON	I know that, Gordon, I read the play last night!
GORDON	Sorry.
MR ATHERTON	I know what I'm doing. Drama is a glorified *invasion game*. People are on different sides, there's conflict and eventually the winner prevails. Now where's Lady Macbeth?

Alexis springs onto the stage.

ALEXIS	Here I am!
MR ATHERTON	Now darlin', when do you first see Macbeth?
ALEXIS	Line fourteen, when he comes back from doing the deed.
MR ATHERTON	Take it from there. *(He blows his whistle.)*
EDWARD	I have done the deed. Didst thou not hear a noise?
ALEXIS	I heard the owl scream and the crickets cry. Did not you speak?
EDWARD	When?
ALEXIS	Now.
EDWARD	As I descended?
ALEXIS	Ay.
EDWARD	Hark! Who lies i' th' second chamber?
ALEXIS	Donalbain.
EDWARD	*(looking at his hands)* This is a sorry sight.
ALEXIS	A foolish thought, to say a sorry sight.
MR ATHERTON	Okay, now, how are you two feeling at this point?
ALEXIS	Fine, thanks.
EDWARD	Terrible. *(Edward glances over to Nigel apologetically.)*
MR ATHERTON	How do your *characters* feel! Together you've done the deed, you two planned it. How do you feel now that it's all kicked in?

ALEXIS	Well, I think Lady Macbeth's the strong one, so she's handling it all probably better than Macbeth.
MR ATHERTON	Are you regretful, Edward?
EDWARD	Yeah.
MR ATHERTON	Do you wish you hadn't done it?
	Pause. Edward looks again at Nigel, he is hesitant.
EDWARD	I'm not sure.
	Nigel stomps out noisily.
MR ATHERTON	You're scared?
EDWARD	Yeah.
MR ATHERTON	Anyway, suddenly there's a knock.
GORDON	*(startled)* In *three pages* there's a knock.
MR ATHERTON	What have I missed?
GORDON	Macbeth's so scared he couldn't finish the job. Lady Macbeth has to go back to the King's chamber and smear the hands of the King's servants with blood.
	Mr Atherton looks confused.
	She's framing them for the murder.
MR ATHERTON	Right. And then there's the knock?
GORDON	Yes.
MR ATHERTON	Let's take it from there.
	Gordon knocks on the stage floor. Roger enters as the porter.
ROGER	Here's a knocking indeed! If a man were a porter of hell-gate he should have old turning the key.
	Gordon knocks again.

Knock, knock, knock. Who's there, i' the name of Beelzebub? Here's a farmer that hanged himself on the expectation of plenty. Come in time; have napkins enow about you; here you'll sweat for't.

Gordon knocks again.

Knock, knock. Who's there, i' th' other devil's name?

Mr Atherton looks increasingly bored.

Faith, here's an equivocator, that could swear in both the scales against either scale, who committed treason enough for God's sake, yet could not equivocate to heaven. O! come in equivocator.

Gordon knocks again.

Knock, knock, knock. Who's there? Faith here's an English tailor . . .

MR ATHERTON	Oh, for goodness sakes *come in!* What is this rubbish? *(He studies the script.)*
ROGER	I've got lots more yet.
MR ATHERTON	*(looking through the pages)* You spout this rubbish for ages, we can't have that. From now on when Macduff knocks just answer the door.
ROGER	But these are my only lines.
GORDON	I believe this character is supposed to lighten the action for a bit.
MR ATHERTON	Well, I don't want him. He's irritating. From now on Macduff knocks, you open the door, Macduff says, 'Is thy master stirring?'
ROGER	That means I'll have no lines at all.
MR ATHERTON	Let's go from the first knock.

Gordon knocks. Roger, looking mortified, opens the door. Gordon enters with Kirsty.

GORDON   Is thy master stirring?

MR ATHERTON   Enter Macbeth!

Edward walks on.

GORDON   Our knocking has awaked him, here he comes.

KIRSTY   Good morrow noble sir.

MR ATHERTON   Who's this? *(He points to Kirsty.)*

GORDON   Lennox, a mate of Macduff's.

MR ATHERTON   Good, right, now why have you suddenly turned up at Macbeth's castle, Macduff?

GORDON   The King asked me to call early for him. We were going to ride back to his place.

MR ATHERTON   And what happens now?

GORDON   Macbeth takes me to the King's chamber and I find him dead.

MR ATHERTON   Take it from there. *(He blows his whistle.)*

GORDON   O horror, horror, horror! Tongue nor heart
Cannot conceive nor name thee!

EDWARD   What's the matter?

GORDON   Confusion now hath made his masterpiece.
Most sacrilegious murder hath broke ope
The Lord's anointed temple, and stole thence
The life o' th' building!

EDWARD   What is't you say—the life?

KIRSTY   Mean you his Majesty?

GORDON   Approach the chamber, and destroy your sight
With a new Gorgon. Do not bid me speak:
See, and then speak yourselves.

Nigel noisily re-enters the room.

MR ATHERTON Alright now are we?

Nigel says nothing. Gordon looks suspicious.

EDWARD *(to Gordon)* What?

GORDON Nothing.

EDWARD Quit staring!

GORDON What's going on? What are you up to?

EDWARD Nothing, Commander!

GORDON Lance Corporal.

MR ATHERTON Stop it. Let's move on.

EDWARD Don't you ever take your hat off?

GORDON Of course.

EDWARD When?

GORDON I remove my hat during many domestic or recreational activities.

MR ATHERTON Right Macduff . . .

ALEXIS Go on! Live dangerously! Take it off!

GORDON No!

MR ATHERTON Cut it out, I said! *(pause)* So Macduff, the players have changed. The King is no longer the King, he's gone. Do you sense a plan underneath it all? Do you smell a rat?

GORDON *(looks at Nigel then Edward)* I'm not sure.

MR ATHERTON Is that the end of Act Two?

GORDON No.

MR ATHERTON What happens now?

GORDON Malcolm and Donalbain flee.

MR ATHERTON Who are they?

GORDON	The King's sons.
KIRSTY	Why?
MR ATHERTON	'Cause they could be implicated, silly.
GORDON	Or maybe they think they might be next.
MR ATHERTON	That's right. And then Act Two ends?
GORDON	Pretty much.
MR ATHERTON	Okay, let's break for five minutes.

All walk off stage apart from Edward. He remains on stage and looks at his hands.

EDWARD   *(to himself)* This is a sorry sight.

The lights fade.

Alexis and Edward are back in the park. This time it is Alexis who is sitting comfortably and Edward who is pacing back and forth.

EDWARD Did you see the way he was looking at me?

ALEXIS Yeah, I know.

EDWARD He hates me now. Why does he hate me? He's still Banquo.

ALEXIS You worry too much.

EDWARD He knows!

ALEXIS I know he knows.

EDWARD I've gotta do something.

ALEXIS He won't squeal. He's your best mate.

EDWARD Not any more.

ALEXIS Relax.

EDWARD I can't relax!

ALEXIS Shhh . . . the warden.

Edward holds his head in his hands.

You're really worried, aren't you?

EDWARD Yes. *(He suddenly looks determined.)* There's only one thing to do.

ALEXIS What?

EDWARD Nigel must . . . go.

Pause.

ALEXIS *You* are a monster! He's your best mate.

EDWARD He's an *obstacle!* *(pause)* You want me to have the limelight, don't you?

ALEXIS Yes.

EDWARD   I'm being *Macbeth*, not Malcolm.

ALEXIS   Well done. *(She puts her arms around him.)* I'm proud of you, in a sick sort of a way.

EDWARD   What about Gordon? He looks at me funny. Maybe he knows as well.

ALEXIS   He looks at *everyone* funny.

Pause.

EDWARD   How am I going to get rid of Nigel?

ALEXIS   I'm sure you'll think of something.

Lights up on the following rehearsal. There is general noise. Mr Atherton arrives and calls them all together on stage.

MR ATHERTON   Right, people, can I have your attention!

The cast hush and face him.

More bad news I'm afraid. We need to find another Banquo. It seems Nigel is now out of the play.

There is a general noise of displeasure.

It seems someone told his mother he was in possession of a pack of nude playing cards. She's grounded him for a month.

More noise, a few gasp.

Let that be a lesson to any of you young boys! Indulging in things like that can have serious repercussions.

SCOTT   Bit harsh though.

MR ATHERTON   That's not for you to judge. Now, obviously, we were going to do Act Three today, but as the first three scenes involve Banquo, who we now don't have, we'll have to start from where Macbeth kills him. Act Three, Scene 4.

SCOTT   Why does he kill him off?

MR ATHERTON   Because he's an obstacle.

SCOTT   To what?

MR ATHERTON   Macbeth's future glory.

GORDON   Also he sussed Macbeth out.

MR ATHERTON   That's right.

SCOTT	What happens?
MR ATHERTON	He hires a couple of people to murder him while he's out on his horse.
DREW	Is the horse okay?
MR ATHERTON	Now the scene we're going to start with is where Macbeth is enjoying his new position as King and entertaining some Lords and other people. However, halfway through the meal Banquo's ghost enters and starts to haunt Macbeth with the guilt of what he's done. Only Macbeth can see him though. Right. Ross, Lennox, Lords, let's have you round the table.

They sit on stage, around a table.

Right Macbeth, take it away. *(He blows his whistle.)*

EDWARD	You know your own degrees, sit down. At first And last, the hearty welcome.
LORDS	Thanks to your Majesty.
EDWARD	Ourself will mingle with society, And play the humble host. Our hostess keeps her state, but in best time We will require her welcome.
ALEXIS	Pronounce it for me sir, to all our friends, For my heart speaks they are welcome.
MR ATHERTON	Enter the First Murderer!

Drew enters and stands in the corner of the room, with a false beard.

Is that necessary, Drew?

DREW	Oh yes.
MR ATHERTON	I thought you were a witch.
DREW	I'm a bearded man.

MR ATHERTON	Why?
AMY	There were too many of us.
MR ATHERTON	Oh. Go ahead, Edward.
EDWARD	*(to Alexis)* See, they encounter thee with their hearts' thanks. *(to the company)* Both sides are even, here I'll sit i' th' midst. *(He goes over to the murderer.)* *(to the company)* Be large in mirth, anon we'll drink a measure The table round. *(to the murderer)* There's blood upon thy face.
DREW	'Tis Banquo's then.
EDWARD	'Tis better thee without than he within. Is he dispatched?
DREW	My lord, his throat is cut; that I did for him.
EDWARD	Thou art the best . . .

Mr Atherton interrupts them with a loud yawn. On opening his eyes, he finds them all staring.

MR ATHERTON	Goes on a bit this, doesn't it? How much more have you got with him, Macbeth?
EDWARD	Couple of pages.
MR ATHERTON	Why don't we skip a bit?
ROGER	Sir, I've calculated that this production of *Macbeth* so far will last approximately ten minutes.
MR ATHERTON	Don't be cheeky! I just want to get through it once. We *will* go back over it. Let's go from . . . Macbeth sees the ghost of Banquo, shall we go from there?

There is a noise at the back of the hall, as someone enters. On seeing the person, Edward's mouth drops, he looks aghast.

Macbeth? *(pause)* Shall we? *(pause)* Edward? From where you see the ghost? *(Mr Atherton turns to see what Edward's staring at.)* Nigel! Thought you were grounded, you naughty little monkey.

Nigel's eyes are fixed firmly on Edward.

NIGEL I left my jacket here.

MR ATHERTON Well, find it quickly and be on your way please. *(He turns back.)* Now, Alexis, what do you do when Macbeth sees the ghost and starts shouting at it, in the midst of your dinner party?

ALEXIS I try and cover for him so the guests don't suspect anything. I tell them he's been feeling unwell?

MR ATHERTON Something like that, yes.

Nigel finds his coat but remains staring at Edward while he rehearses.

Action! *(He blows his whistle.)*

KIRSTY Here is a place reserved, sir.

EDWARD Where?

KIRSTY *(pointing to an empty chair)* Here my good lord.

Edward becomes aware of Nigel observing him. He looks uncomfortable.

KIRSTY What is't that moves your Highness?

MR ATHERTON Now Macbeth, this is where you see the ghost.

EDWARD Which of you have done this?

LORDS What, my good lord?

EDWARD *(to the ghost)* Thou canst not say I did it; never shake

Thy gory locks at me.

SCOTT	Gentlemen, rise, his Highness is not well.

During Alexis's next section, Edward keeps glancing round and becomes increasingly uncomfortable with Nigel's presence.

ALEXIS	Sit worthy friends. My lord is often thus,
	And hath been from his youth. Pray you keep seat,
	The fit is momentary, upon a thought
	He will again be well. If much you note him,
	You shall offend him, and extend his passion.
	Feed, and regard him not.

Suddenly Edward shouts at Nigel who is in the darkness.

EDWARD	Leave me alone! It wasn't me! I didn't do it!

Nigel remains silent. The cast look confused.

MR ATHERTON	Edward, what on earth's the matter with you? Who are you talking to?
EDWARD	He knows! He knows!
MR ATHERTON	I'm damned if I know.

Alexis springs forward and tries to manhandle Edward back into the scene. Gordon looks suspicious.

ALEXIS	He's okay. He's just a little anxious at the moment. It's the character, it's going to his head. He'll be alright, just give him a few minutes.

The tea ladies enter noisily and distract everyone's attention. Nigel slips off.

MR ATHERTON	Bit early aren't we girls?
SUE	It's now or never, Meg's got a hair appointment.
MEG	*(appeasing)* Sorry!

Edward looks relieved to see Meg.

EDWARD	Thank God. *(He rushes over to the trolley, and tries to talk to her discreetly.)* You need to tell me more!
MEG	About what?
EDWARD	About what you said.
MEG	What did I say? I don't remember.
EDWARD	About the *greater things*. You said this part will lead me to *greater things*.
MEG	Did I?
EDWARD	*(looking at her in disbelief)* Yes. You did.
MEG	*(apologetically)* I tell you, I'd forget me head if it wasn't screwed on.
EDWARD	Well?
MEG	I'd have to see the leaves again.
EDWARD	The same ones?
MEG	Preferably.
EDWARD	I gave the cup back to you.
MEG	That was silly.
EDWARD	Why?
MEG	Well, 'cause I washed it up. What do you think they pay me for?
EDWARD	I know! I'll do it again!

He grabs a cup of tea, and starts gulping. Sue and Lil look on, disapprovingly.

MEG	Careful! That's hot!

Edward fills it half with milk, and continues drinking.

Like it milky, do you?

He finishes it and hands her the cup.

No. Sorry.

EDWARD   What?

MEG   I can't see nothing this time.

EDWARD   *(outraged)* Why not?

MEG   The leaves just aren't talking.

EDWARD   *(shouts)* Make them!

MEG   *(annoyed)* I'm sorry.

EDWARD   Wait. I'll try it again.

He grabs another cup of tea, adds milk and starts gulping. Meg shakes her head. Mr Atherton comes over to Edward.

MR ATHERTON   Alright, Edward?

EDWARD   *(grunts)* Umm.

MR ATHERTON   Nothing bothering you?

EDWARD   *(lowering the cup with care)* No.

He stares, madly, at the bottom of his cup, then slowly hands it to Meg, with enormous care.

MR ATHERTON   I see. Well, as long as you're okay.

Mr Atherton goes. We hear him speak to the cast.

He's fine.

Meg looks at his cup. She shakes her head.

EDWARD   More!

MEG   I think you've had enough!

EDWARD   I need to know!

He grabs someone else's from the trolley, downs it and hands it to her.

MEG	Ah!
EDWARD	Ah?
MEG	Yes. This is good. I see something.
EDWARD	Thank you. Thank you. Thank you.
MEG	Don't thank me yet. You don't know what it says. *(She studies the cup.)* You're going to do very well. People will compare you to the greats.
EDWARD	They will?
MEG	Oh yes. Prepare for stardom, young man!
EDWARD	Really?

Meg nods, smiling.

	What *are* the greater things?
MEG	More parts. Television parts. Film offers. Celebrity parties.
EDWARD	That's fantastic!
MEG	Shhh. Don't tell anyone.
EDWARD	I won't.

She looks again at the cup.

MEG	Hold! Hold!
EDWARD	What?
MEG	A warning!
EDWARD	What?
MEG	It's difficult to make out.
EDWARD	Try. You must.
MEG	Yes. I see it. *(She looks up slowly.)* Beware, beware, he who has red hair!
EDWARD	Red?
MEG	Ay.

EDWARD   You mean like ginger?

MEG   Ay.

EDWARD   *(fearful)* Is this person going to spoil it all?

MEG   Ay. Beware, beware, he who has red hair.

The tea ladies start to go.

SUE   I'm sure that's just *general* advice she'd give to
          anyone, darling.

MEG   Yeah. Don't dwell on it, love.

They go.

Edward and Alexis are together at the park. Edward paces behind Alexis, who has a pen and paper and appears to be engrossed in some kind of calculation.

ALEXIS   Lee Russell?

EDWARD   On holiday for three weeks.

ALEXIS   Excellent. *(She ticks him off on the paper.)*
Barny Chandler?

EDWARD   Hates drama. Won't come near us.

She ticks him off.

ALEXIS   Adrian Gibbs?

EDWARD   He's not ginger.

ALEXIS   Isn't he?

Edward shakes his head. She ticks him off.

Peter Ford?

EDWARD   He's a year *seven*, I don't think he's gonna pose much of a threat. I could fit him in me pocket.

Pause.

ALEXIS   I think that's it then.

Edward throws his hands up in victory.

EDWARD   Yes! It's mine! No one can stop me now!

ALEXIS   Certainly looks that way.

EDWARD   I am invincible!

ALEXIS   Have you done the year tens?

EDWARD   *(dismissing)* Yes, yes, yes. It feels so amazing. I am there. I am there!

ALEXIS   Are you sure you've done the year tens?

Pause. Edward looks annoyed at her lack of euphoria.

EDWARD   There's a couple that could be a problem, but I got Charlie Slater taking care of them.

ALEXIS   What's he gonna do?

EDWARD   Dunno. Whatever he normally does. He just said, 'I'll make sure they don't develop an interest in Drama.'

Alexis suddenly looks concerned.

ALEXIS   They probably wouldn't anyway. I do hope he's not too rough on them.

EDWARD   Not developing a conscience?

ALEXIS   I'm not that hard.

EDWARD   I'm just making sure.

ALEXIS   Are you sure you're not getting a little obsessed with this?

EDWARD   You've changed your tune.

She looks uncomfortable, then confesses.

ALEXIS   I got a bit worried about you at rehearsal today. The veins in your neck were bulging. You looked like a psycho.

EDWARD   Sorry about that. *(He thinks to himself.)* I've got to do something about Gordon.

ALEXIS   *(worried)* What?

EDWARD   He knows too much.

ALEXIS   He doesn't know anything!

EDWARD   I've got to do something! I've got to be sure!

ALEXIS   Pretty soon, there won't be a cast left!

EDWARD   We'll manage.

Pause.

ALEXIS   Edward, I'm not sure I like you as much as I did. I'm going.

EDWARD   *(calls after her)* What do you expect? There's a lot at stake here!

Lights up on the rehearsal hall. No one is present apart from Timothy, sitting by himself on the stage. Suddenly Gordon, in truly heroic style, comes bursting through the door, with tremendous energy.

GORDON   Here you are!

Pause.

TIMOTHY   *(confused)* Here I am.

Gordon strides over to him.

GORDON   I need to speak to you before the others get here. Bad things are going down, Tim. Corruption is rife in this seemingly *cosy* little gang and it must be stopped.

TIMOTHY   What are you talking about? What must be stopped?

GORDON   *Him*, Timothy. *He* must be stopped.

TIMOTHY   Who?

GORDON   Edward.

TIMOTHY   Edward!

GORDON   *(paces up and down the stage)* He is behind everything! He's out of control!

TIMOTHY   Gordon, you're starting to scare me.

GORDON   First Mrs Painter, then he knocks you off the throne, then he gets Nigel out of the way, he knew too much, and he's just tried to rub me out of the picture.

TIMOTHY   What do you mean?

Pause. Gordon struggles to tell the story without getting angry.

GORDON	He offered my help to working mothers.
TIMOTHY	Eh?
GORDON	He put my name down to help out at the village hall, every day after school.
TIMOTHY	Doing what?
GORDON	Helping to supervise . . . *a crèche*.
TIMOTHY	No!
GORDON	All the mothers phoned the headmaster to say what an outstanding example I was to the school . . . Broke my heart letting all those good people down. Calculating tyrant knew I wouldn't find that easy . . . but he made one mistake . . . he *thought* I'd find it impossible. I'm on his trail now, he's *mine*.
TIMOTHY	But how can you be certain it's him?

Gordon gets out a piece of paper from his jacket and thrusts it in front of Timothy's face.

| GORDON | It's amazing what you find if you go through the rubbish for long enough. |

He hands the piece of paper to Timothy, who reads.

GORDON	Recognise the hand?
TIMOTHY	*(reading)* 'Dear Mr Atherton, would you be so kind as to tell the group there was a mistake on the cast list yes . . . sterday,' spelt with two S's. 'Tim mustn't play Macbeth, it should be Edward.' This is Edward's writing.
GORDON	Bingo! I'll tell you something else. I saw him win those dirty cards at the fair an'all. They weren't *Nigel's*. He didn't have to have them either, he could have had some jelly babies. I don't miss a thing.

TIMOTHY	What are you going to do?
GORDON	What are *we* going to do? He knocked you off the throne! You should be Macbeth! You should be the star!

Pause. Timothy lowers his head.

TIMOTHY	I can't be a star, Gordon, I'm not star quality.
GORDON	What is this?
TIMOTHY	Edward's much better than I would be, anyway.
GORDON	You're not going to let him get away with it.
TIMOTHY	What am I supposed to do? Muck up the whole thing by demanding to be Macbeth again? Then I'll be rubbish and people will wish Edward was back.
GORDON	You will not be rubbish! Get up!
TIMOTHY	What?
GORDON	I said get up!

Timothy gets up. Gordon finds a page in his script and hands it to Timothy.

Before he kills the King, Macbeth sees a vision of a dagger hovering in front of him. What are you thinking, Macbeth?

TIMOTHY	What?
GORDON	Come on, Tim!

Timothy closes his eyes and thinks hard.

TIMOTHY	What does this mean?
GORDON	Good.
TIMOTHY	Is it a sign, or my own imagination?
GORDON	That's right.
TIMOTHY	Shall I take it or not?

GORDON	Now read.

Timothy opens his eyes and starts to read.

TIMOTHY	Is this a dagger which I see before me,
GORDON	You sound like you're only mildly curious. You're in turmoil!
TIMOTHY	Is this a dagger which I see before me,
GORDON	Better!
TIMOTHY	The handle toward my hand?
GORDON	See it! See it!

Timothy fixes his eyes on an imaginary dagger and begins to reach for it.

TIMOTHY	Come let me clutch thee.
GORDON	I like that! Keep that! Say it again!
TIMOTHY	Come let me clutch thee. I have thee not, and yet I see thee still. Art thou not, fatal vision, sensible To feeling as to sight? Or art thou but A *dagger* of the mind . . .

Timothy pauses, then steps out of character. He looks amazed. Gordon looks impressed.

That was quite good.

GORDON	Yes it was.

Suddenly voices are heard in the corridor.

Promise me one thing.

TIMOTHY	What?
GORDON	That you'll learn his lines.
TIMOTHY	Whose?

GORDON	Macbeth's!
TIMOTHY	Why?
GORDON	I'm getting you your throne back. You *will be* the King of this show.
TIMOTHY	There's so many though! There's loads of them! Who's gonna play Malcolm?
GORDON	Talk to Nigel. Get him to learn Malcolm. It'll give him something to do while he's in jail.
TIMOTHY	I don't know, Gordon.
GORDON	Promise! Then leave the rest to me.

Pause.

TIMOTHY	Okay.

The rest of the group come bursting through the door. Mr Atherton makes his way to the stage, the others gather before him.

MR ATHERTON	Right, we all here? Good.

Mr Atherton hears the swish of a sword behind him. He turns to see Edward on stage having an imaginary sword fight. He looks in tremendous high spirits, bursting with energy and confidence.

Umm . . . Edward, will you be joining the rest of us?

EDWARD	Oh no. I am in a league of my own! *(He continues fighting.)* You couldn't get near me. No one can. No one can touch me. *(He mimes killing his victim, then looks at his audience and bows.)* What do you think?
MR ATHERTON	Yes, very energetic.

Edward parades the stage.

EDWARD	Thank you! Thank you! No, you're too kind!

MR ATHERTON	Come and sit down!

Edward eventually sits.

Right, I thought we'd start from the beginning of Act Four. Macbeth goes to see the witches a second time.

EDWARD	Boring!
AMY	No it's not!
ZARA	We've got important things to tell you.
EDWARD	Like what?
KIRSTY	Like none of woman born can harm thee.
EDWARD	I already know that. Macbeth already knows that.
DREW	No he doesn't.
MR ATHERTON	He doesn't, Edward. Stop being so pig-headed.
EDWARD	Alright, none of woman born can harm me! And that must mean no one, right? 'Cause everyone's born of a woman.
GORDON	That's what he thinks.
EDWARD	So that means he's invincible! I am invincible!
GORDON	Until the end.
EDWARD	What?
GORDON	Until you realise I was born through a caesarean section.
EDWARD	A what?
ZARA	That's where you come out through the tummy.
KIRSTY	Abdomen.
GORDON	So I wasn't truly born of a woman. You see.

Edward looks disappointed.

Hadn't banked on that, had you?

EDWARD	It's not a problem.

GORDON Well, it is, 'cause I end up killing you.

EDWARD Do you?

He rifles through his script and finds the scene. Gordon is enjoying the whole experience.

GORDON Notice how your confidence starts to dwindle when you hear the line 'Macduff was from his mother's womb
Untimely ripped.'

Edward looks annoyed.

All that confidence, all that boundless energy. Zapped! Just like that. What does Macbeth end up saying to Macduff? Edward? What does that line just there say? *(He points to the text.)*

EDWARD *(quietly)* I'll not fight with thee.

GORDON I'll not fight with thee! He turns into a coward!

EDWARD *(to Mr Atherton, confused)* I thought I won.

MR ATHERTON Oh no.

Pause.

EDWARD Oh well, I don't care, I've still got more lines! I'm still the centrepiece of the whole play! I mean they don't call the play Macduff! Do they! Ha ha! Why don't we move straight on to Act Five, Scene 3, where Macbeth realises no one can harm him. And he stands alone against thousands of soldiers! Action! *(He grabs Mr Atherton's whistle from the stage and blows it.)*

MR ATHERTON Hey! No one blows that whistle but me, young man. I don't care who you're playing. And may I remind you who is directing this piece? We'll do the scenes I suggest! Act Four, Scene 3. Macduff and Malcolm.

The witches grumble.

MR ATHERTON   Don't worry girls. We'll go back and do your bit.

Edward sighs. Gordon and Timothy make their way to the stage.

What happens in this scene, Gordon?

GORDON   Macduff tells Malcolm what a scheming rat Macbeth is. How he *usurped* him from the throne, that he is the man responsible for all the *torment* that has been endured. Macduff tries to get Malcolm to return to Scotland to fight Macbeth and become King. Malcolm pretends he wouldn't make a good king but then agrees.

MR ATHERTON   Let's see Malcolm's first response. Go from line forty-five. *(He blows his whistle.)*

TIMOTHY   When I shall tread upon the tyrant's head,
Or wear it on my sword, yet my poor country
Shall have more vices than it had before,
More suffer, and more sundry ways than ever,
By him that shall succeed.

GORDON   What should he be?

TIMOTHY   It is myself I mean; in whom I know
All the particulars of vice so grafted,
That, when they shall be opened, black Macbeth
Will seem as pure as snow, and the poor state
Esteem him as a lamb, being compared
With my confineless harms.

MR ATHERTON   *(impressed)* That was nice, Tim. You're coming on.

TIMOTHY   Thank you.

EDWARD	*(sarcastic)* Splendid Tim! Absolutely super! Couldn't fault it! Marvellous! Shall we do my scene now?
	The entire cast look at Edward with utter dislike.
MR ATHERTON	No. We won't. We will do . . . Lady Macbeth's sleepwalking scene.
EDWARD	Tiny problem there, old boy, Alexis ain't here.
MR ATHERTON	*(looking around)* Where is she?
EDWARD	*(unperturbed)* I do believe she may have abandoned the show.
MR ATHERTON	What? You can't be serious!
EDWARD	Alas, I'm afraid I am. *(He lunges forward with his sword towards an imaginary enemy.)* Be gone villain!
MR ATHERTON	Edward! Will you *stop* doing that!
	Edward stops.
MR ATHERTON	*(alarmed)* Now, does anyone know if this is true?
LARA	I think it is. She said the whole experience was starting to make her feel nauseous.
MR ATHERTON	Well, this is terrible.
	Pause. There is quiet.
EDWARD	Well, we may as well carry on. Shall we do my scene?
	Pause.
MR ATHERTON	*(conceding)* Very well.
EDWARD	Let's go! Lara! You're up!
	He bounds to the stage and continues sword fighting an imaginary enemy. Lara comes on stage and tries to hand him a scroll.

EDWARD	Bring me no more reports, let them fly all.
	Till Birnam wood remove to Dunsinane,
	I cannot taint with fear. What's the boy Malcolm?
	Was he not born of woman? The spirits that know
	All mortal consequences have pronounced me thus:
	'Fear not, Macbeth: no man that's born of woman
	Shall e'er have power upon thee.' Then fly, false thanes,
	And mingle with the English epicures.
	The mind I sway by, and the heart I bear,
	Shall never sag with doubt, nor shake with fear.

Enter Lara as servant.

	The devil damn thee black, thou cream-faced loon.
	What gott'st thou that goose look?
LARA	There is ten thousand—
EDWARD	Geese, villain?
LARA	Soldiers sir.
EDWARD	Go prick thy face, and over-red thy fear,
	Thou lily-livered boy. What soldiers, patch?
	Death of thy soul, those linen cheeks of thine
	Are counsellors to fear. What soldiers, whey-face?

Lara mimes looking from the window.

LARA	The English force, so please you.
EDWARD	Take thy face hence.

Lara goes. Edward looks overjoyed.

	What do you think?
MR ATHERTON	*(grudgingly)* Yes, good, Edward. Not bad at all.
EDWARD	Thank you! *(He parades the stage again.)* Thank you!
	Thank you! One and all.

He bows. As he does so, the tea ladies enter with their trolley. Behind them Charlie Slater tries to sneak in, unnoticed. He carries a note in his hand which he tries to give Edward discreetly. Gordon sees him, however, and pounces.

GORDON   Oy!

He runs over and grabs Charlie by the lapels.

CHARLIE   Let me go!

GORDON   What's your game?

CHARLIE   I haven't done nothing. I'm just leaving a note for someone. No crime against that.

Gordon grabs the note.

GORDON   And who is this for?

Edward's confidence is suddenly dented. He shakes his head at Charlie, but it's too late.

CHARLIE   Edward.

GORDON   I see. *(He opens the note.)*

CHARLIE   Oy! That's personal!

Charlie tries to grab the note but Gordon's too quick.

GORDON   'Ed. All ginger-haired males taken care of. Charlie.'

Meg shrieks.

EDWARD   I don't know what he's talking about!

MEG   What have I done! *(to Edward)* I told you not to take it too seriously!

Heads fly from person to person. No one understands the exchange.

SUE   Meg, you're awful. You filled his head with so many images of glory, it's no wonder it's driven him to this.

MR ATHERTON	What is everyone talking about?
EDWARD	I don't know.
GORDON	I think I'm starting to. So, ginger is the big stumbling block, is it?
LIL	That was the only thing that could stand in his way.
EDWARD	Shhh!
MR ATHERTON	Will someone please tell me what's going on!
EDWARD	Yes. I agree.

Gordon has a plan.

GORDON	It's okay. I'm sure it's just a misunderstanding. Charlie, I'm sure all the note meant was that you were looking after the ginger-haired members of the school, 'cause they do tend to get bullied more. So you really were *taking care of them*. Isn't that right?
CHARLIE	*(can't believe his luck)* Yeah, that's right.
GORDON	And I'm sure the only reason you wanted to give Edward this note is because he too cares a great deal and wants to know that they are okay.

Edward looks suspicious but goes along with it.

EDWARD	Yeah, that's right.
MEG	*(looks relieved)* That's alright then, you had me worried for a moment.

Pause.

MR ATHERTON	*(looks bewildered)* Well, I'm still rather confused, but as long as everyone's happy. Let's break for tea.

Everyone moves off in various directions, some queue at the trolley. The spotlight beams on Gordon.

GORDON	*(to himself)* The stage is set. Vengeance is mine.

Fade.

As a low eerie light comes up, the three tea ladies are sitting around their tea-trolley as at the beginning of the play, lazily drinking tea. The urn bubbles away in the background.

LIL   So, time moves on, eh?

Pause.

SUE   Yep. Would have thought they'd had enough of our tea after three weeks.

MEG   Is it that long?

SUE   Umm.

LIL   Wonder what happened to that nice little boy who left?

SUE   Oh, you mean *naughty Nigel!*

They laugh.

LIL   Such a quiet little thing. Who'd have thought he was such a lady's man?

SUE   Well, cardboard ones don't answer back, do they?

LIL   They replaced him with one of the others, they've got two parts now.

SUE   That's not right, is it?

LIL AND MEG   No.

SUE   Poor kid won't know whether he's coming or going.

Pause.

MEG   Did they find someone else for that Lady Macbeth?

SUE   Yeah. One of the witches is doing it now.

MEG   Really? So now they're one witch short?

SUE   Looks that way.

LIL	Started off with four, now they only got two.
MEG	What they gonna do? Make do with two?
LIL	Can't do that, can they Sue? Everyone knows there's supposed to be three of 'em.
SUE	Well, they better find someone soon, curtain goes up tomorrow night.
LIL	I did hear, the director couldn't find anyone ugly enough. Apparently he wants someone who looks like the back end of a cow.
MEG	Charming.
LIL	You know, to be the leader of them.
MEG	Trouble is, you can't really advertise for someone like that, can you?
LIL	*(whispers)* I heard him say he's got someone in mind.
MEG	Who?
LIL	I don't know. *(whispers)* Apparently, whoever it is, he's gonna ask her today, if she'll read the part tonight.
SUE	What, at the dress?
MEG	Bit late, innit?
LIL	She'll never be able to learn the words.
SUE	Better than nothing though, I s'pose.
MEG	*(starts laughing)* 'Ere, I hope she ain't too ugly. I won't be able to keep a straight face.
LIL	Meg.
SUE	You just serve the tea and don't be so silly.
MEG	Honestly, I'm terrible, once I get started. All I'm gonna be able to see is the back end of a cow! *(She continues laughing.)*
	Fade.

Darkness fills the stage. Suddenly, loud, deep rumbles of thunder echo round the whole auditorium. Fierce flashes of lightning briefly illuminate a backdrop showing a distant plain, also three strange figures crouched together round a cauldron, in the middle of the stage. A low light now shines out of the cauldron illuminating two of the witches' faces. The third witch is completely covered with a blanket. Dry ice rises slowly from the floor as the first witch speaks.

KIRSTY   When shall we three meet again
         In thunder, lightning, or in rain?

ZARA   When the hurlyburly's done,
         When the battle's lost and won.

         Silence.

MR ATHERTON   Third Witch! It's your line!

The third witch wrestles with a black shawl that she has wrapped around her head. Eventually she manages to throw it off. Underneath, it is Meg.

MEG   Sorry. I couldn't see under that blanket.

MR ATHERTON   Meg, it's *supposed* to be over your shoulders.

MEG   Why?

MR ATHERTON   Because I want the audience to see your face.

MEG   *(under her breath)* Yeah, I bet you do.

MR ATHERTON   Can we do it again please?

The same effects are repeated.

KIRSTY   When shall we three meet again
         In thunder, lightning, or in rain?

ZARA   When the hurlyburly's done,
         When the battle's lost and won.

MEG	*(reads from quite a large sheet of paper)* That will be ere the set of sun.
KIRSTY	Where the place?
ZARA	Upon the heath.
MEG	*(reading)* There to meet with Macbeth.
MR ATHERTON	*(interrupts)* Right, okay. Not too bad. Um . . . Meg, where's that script I gave you?
MEG	Over there.
MR ATHERTON	Well, what have you got there?

Meg shows him the sheet of paper.

MEG	My lines. I wrote them out bigger.
MR ATHERTON	A lot bigger. Is that paper A2?
MEG	I don't know. Don't baffle me with jargon, Mr Atherton. I just know it helps me see the words. I can't help it if I got bad eyes, especially in this light.
MR ATHERTON	Alright, not to worry.
MEG	I mean I'm doing you a favour here.
MR ATHERTON	I know, I know. It's just that I'm a bit concerned that our production of Macbeth opens with one of the witches looking like she's reading a newspaper.
MEG	Apologies. *(She walks off the set in a huff.)*
MR ATHERTON	It's not a problem, honestly. Right, what's next? Ah, I know. Macbeth and Macduff meet on the plain. *(He shouts to the cast.)* This is the last one folks, once we've finished the tech, the dress will commence immediately, so be ready! *(He puts earphones on, with a microphone enabling him to talk to the lighting and sound technicians, who are in various places throughout the hall.)* Right, this is the big one then. Can you hear me? These things aren't

working. Mr Lighting and Mr Sound? Can you hear me?

We hear their response through the headphones.

MR LIGHTING   Yeah.

MR SOUND   Yeah.

MR ATHERTON   Right, good, now this is the big scene. Macduff finally meets Macbeth on the plain. I want an eerie atmosphere. Give me the sound of a low wind gushing through the trees. It's on a tape there somewhere.

Suddenly Elvis Presley's 'Hound Dog' comes bursting through the speakers.

No. That's not it.

The wind noise comes on now, but very loud.

Yes. Turn it down! (pause) Turn it down! It's not that windy, that's just silly.

It's turned down.

That's better. Now a dim light from the back so Gordon and Edward are in silhouette.

A spotlight comes on, lighting them harshly from the front. Edward is downstage centre, facing the audience, Gordon is about ten feet behind Edward. Both are in full costume. They squint as the light is turned on.

Is that a silhouette! Are they in silhouette! From the back!

The spotlight goes off. The correct light now comes on from the back, making the boys look like two daunting figures.

Good, right, plot that!

Pause.

GORDON   This is it then. I've been waiting for this moment
         for quite some time. Do you remember what
         happens here? I tell you about my birth, you cower
         and then I defeat you.

EDWARD   Then *I* get a standing ovation.

GORDON   Don't count your chickens before they hatch.

EDWARD   Too late for you to stop me. Tomorrow night's *my*
         night. It's written in the stars.

GORDON   Let's just wait and see, I have one last card to play.
         (He shouts to Timothy, who is in the wings.) Are you
         ready to take his place, Tim?

TIMOTHY *(off stage)* Ready!

EDWARD   Take whose place?

GORDON   *(to Timothy)* You know his lines?

TIMOTHY *(off stage)* I know 'em all.

EDWARD   Whose lines?

GORDON   *(smiles) Your* lines, Edward.

EDWARD   My lines are staying right where they are, with me.

GORDON   Where's Nigel, Tim?

TIMOTHY *(off stage)* Right here!

EDWARD   *(confused)* Nigel! What's going on?

*Suddenly Mr Atherton's voice booms over the
microphone.*

MR ATHERTON   Good, right, well I think we can now continue.
              Ready, team! *(pause)* Action!

GORDON   *(quietly)* May the best man win.

EDWARD *(begins)* Why should I play the Roman fool, and die
On mine own sword? Whiles I see lives, the gashes
Do better upon them.

GORDON *(from behind)* Turn, hell-hound, turn!

EDWARD Of all men else I have avoided thee:
But get thee back, my soul is too much charged
With blood of thine already.

GORDON I have no words:
My voice is in my sword, thou bloodier villain
Than terms can give thee out!

They fight with swords. Both look strong.

EDWARD Thou losest labour:
As easy mayst thou the intrenchant air
With thy keen sword impress, as make me bleed.
Let fall thy blade on vulnerable crests;
I bear a charmed life, which must not yield
To one of woman born.

GORDON Despair thy charm,
And let the angel whom thou still hast served
Tell thee, *(quietly) Are you ready?* Macduff was from
his mother's womb
Untimely ripped!

*Gordon rips off his helmet to reveal a staggeringly bright
red head of hair. He flicks his head and lets it fall about
his ears. There are gasps from the cast. Edward's mouth
has dropped and he only manages to point, bewildered.*

EDWARD *(finally managing to speak)* It's gin . . . ger.

GORDON Yes. I thought for the fiery Scot Macduff is, I'd show
my true colours. *(pause)* How 'bout you show yours?

EDWARD *(still pointing, he looks out to Mr Atherton, as if asking
for help)* It's gin . . . ger.

MR ATHERTON	Edward, what on earth is the matter with you?

Pause. Edward looks back to Gordon, who is standing proud as ever.

	Edward! Pull yourself together, it's your line!
EDWARD	*(trying to get it back)* Accursed be that tongue that tells me so. Umm . . . *(Pause. He frantically searches his mind for the next line.)* Line!
PROMPT	For it hath . . .
EDWARD	For it hath . . . *(Pause. He looks increasingly hysterical.)* What's my line!
GORDON	*(prompts)* Cowed my better part of man.
EDWARD	Cowed . . . my better part of man. *(pause)* It's all gone! I can't remember anything!
MR ATHERTON	*(angry)* This is the dress rehearsal!
EDWARD	Umm . . . Then yield thee coward!
GORDON	That's my line.
MR ATHERTON	That's Macduff's line!
EDWARD	Alright!

Edward looks around for support. He is desperate and alone. Eventually he slowly removes his helmet and throws it to the ground. He unstraps his belt and sword and lets them fall. Gordon slowly raises his clenched fists in victory as Edward exits.

MR ATHERTON	What's going on? This is the dress rehearsal. What is going on?

Timothy slowly walks on to the stage, picks up Edward's sword and belt and, ceremoniously, starts to attach it.

	Tim, what are you doing?
GORDON	Hail, King, for so thou art!
MR ATHERTON	No he isn't!

Gordon walks across to where Edward's helmet lies on the stage. He picks it up and holds it high in the air.

GORDON   Behold where stands
Th' usurper's cursed head!

MR ATHERTON   Um . . . Hello? Gordon?

Gordon, oblivious to Mr Atherton's comments, walks across to where Timothy is kneeling, as if waiting to be knighted. The rest of the cast, curious as to what is going on, begin to gather visibly on each side of the stage. As Gordon continues with his lines, he places Edward's helmet on Timothy's head.

GORDON   The time is free.
I see thee compassed with thy kingdom's pearl,
That speak my salutation with their minds;
Whose voices I desire aloud with mine:

MR ATHERTON   *(standing up and shouting furiously at Gordon)* Hey!
Will you tell me what's going on! Where's Edward!
And if Tim is now Macbeth, who's playing Malcolm?
Eh! Answer me that!

GORDON   *(looking to the wings and stretching out his arms invitingly)* Hail, King of Scotland!

Again with a sense of great ceremony, Nigel walks out on to the stage, dressed in crown and robe, and stands proudly in the centre.

MR ATHERTON   Nigel!

GORDON   *(looking to the cast for support)* Come on! It's your line!

Pause. The cast look round at each other.

ALL   Hail, King of Scotland!

Blackout.

The End

Activities

Note

The letters and numbers next to each task indicate which aspects of the *Framework for Teaching English: Years 7, 8 and 9* the exercise relates to. It is difficult to be wholly precise and accurate with this, as many exercises do not fit snugly into one category, but instead touch on a few aspects of several categories. Therefore the letters and numbers are only a general guide.

The first number, 7, 8 or 9, shows which Year group the exercise is for. The letter or letters next to this represent which category within the framework the exercise relates to. For example:

WL = Word Level
SL = Sentence Level (not Speaking & Listening)
R = Reading
W = Writing
S = Speaking
L = Listening
GD = Group Discussion
D = Drama

The final number, after the letters, represents which unit within the category the exercise relates to.

For instance, if a task is labelled 7W6 and 8R3 it covers Unit 6 of the Year 7 Writing framework and Unit 3 of the Year 8 Reading framework.

Scene 1

Focus on the Scene

Task 1: 7R2, 7R12, 7R14, 8R4, 9R14, 9W11, 9W5

Read the opening of Scene 1 again. What kind of atmosphere do you think the writer is trying to convey with just the opening scene directions, before any actual dialogue is spoken? Here is the section again.

As a low eerie light comes up, three tea ladies are sitting around a tea-trolley quietly drinking tea. Behind them on the trolley an urn bubbles away like a cauldron. Meg, one of the ladies, is studying the bottom of a cup with great concentration.

Find three words or phrases in this short section which you think most help us to feel the atmosphere, as we visualise the scene. Share your ideas with the class. Try to explain why you feel the words or phrases you have chosen communicate the scene particularly well.

As an exercise, try rewriting the opening scene directions in a different way, still making it as atmospheric as possible, and being as descriptive and detailed as you can.

Task 2: 7W6, 7W14, 8W6

As a short writing exercise, using the information given to you in Scene 1, imagine you have to write a very short description of each of the tea ladies for the Character List at the beginning of the play. Use their responses, their general tone, what they say about themselves, and what others say about them to support your description. Remember, you do not have to write in full sentences for this type of description. For example, it could just say:

Character X – Mid-forties, short, haggard looking, with a fast mouth. The type who likes to moan.

Share your ideas with the class. Discuss differences of opinion. Try to support your interpretation with references to the text.

Try putting your interpretation of the character into practice by reading the scene in small groups. Use what you said about them in your description to inform your reading of the part. After trying to read the character in a certain way, you may decide you were wrong about them. You could perhaps present each scene to the class. After several groups have read it, decide as a class whose ideas you think worked best for which character.

Focus on *Macbeth*

Read Act One, Scenes 1 and 3 of *Macbeth*

Which parts of these scenes tell us most about the characters of the three witches? To help you, study these questions in groups.

- Why do you think the weather is an important factor in when they decide to meet again? (Scene 1, line 1)
- What does it suggest two of the sisters had been up to, before Scene 3 began? (Scene 3, lines 1–10)
- What does the story the first witch recites to the others tell us about her character? (Scene 3, lines 4–29)
- What do the responses of the other witches to the story tell us about *their* characters? (Scene 3, lines 11 and 13)
- How do you think the witch intends to use the pilot's thumb she has obtained? (line 28)

Share your answers with the class.

Discuss what you think the similarities and the differences are between the tea ladies in Scene 1 of *Macbeth on the Loose*, and the witches in Act One, Scenes 1 and 3 of *Macbeth*. In groups, try creating a table and listing your answers, as below.

Similarities	Differences
Both involved in supernatural things	Witches more nasty

Once you have listed as many things as you can, share your ideas with other groups. See who has produced the most extensive list. Add to your lists accordingly.

Task 3: 7R2, 7W8, 7D17

One of the differences you may have drawn out from the two scenes is that much of what the witches say is written in *rhyming couplets*. This tends to give the speaker of the lines quite a defined way of pronouncing them. In small groups, try reading the scene paying particular attention to the rhyming scheme Shakespeare has introduced into it.

After reading the scene discuss the following questions.

- How does it affect the way you deliver the lines?
- Does it make the reading easier?
- Does it make the reading more enjoyable?
- Does it help you to feel like the character?
- Do you think it helps communicate anything to the audience or listener?

Discuss your ideas together and feed back your conclusions to the class.

Drama Activities

1 Imaginary Scenarios 7D15, 8D15 and 16, 9D12

Sometimes a really good way of helping us to understand a character and get a good idea of what they are like is by imagining them in other situations and thinking about how they might respond.

In groups, try putting the tea ladies into one of the following situations and devise an *improvisation* based on what you think they are like, and how you think they would respond. It is important to ensure that all your responses within the scene are consistent with the character you are playing.

- You are all on a plane when the pilot announces that due to engine failure he will have to make an emergency landing. How does your character react?
- You are all in a shop when suddenly an armed robber rushes in, holds the place up with a gun and demands that you get on the floor. How does your character respond?
- You are at a zoo when you suddenly notice someone has fallen into a crocodile-infested lake, and is crying for help. What would your character do?

2 Moulding 7D15

This is a very useful technique for ensuring that a visual image is as expressive as it can be. In small groups, begin by allowing one person to direct the others into forming a freeze-frame for the opening of either *Macbeth on the Loose* or *Macbeth*. This person is the *moulder*.

(A freeze-frame is a moment of action from a piece of drama, frozen with the actors in certain physical positions and with certain facial expressions.)

Once the moulder has made the *general* image they are after, they then stand back and view it to see if improvements could be made by adding more detail or subtlety of expression. They may ask people to stand differently, change their facial expression, use the space differently, whatever is needed to make a really effective visual image.

Once this has been done, and the class have evaluated its effectiveness, *guest moulders* can be invited to change the image if they feel they could do a better job. Take turns in having a go. Decide whose ideas you think are most effective in communicating the scene.

Scene 2

Focus on the Scene

Task 1: 7R2, 8R4

This is the first time we are introduced to two of the main characters in the play, Edward and Nigel. Although they are apparently the best of friends, they are very different in terms of character.

Find five parts in the scene where the differences between their characters are most clearly seen.

Share your answers with the class.

Now look at the following words and decide which characteristic belongs to which character, Edward or Nigel. There are not necessarily any right or wrong answers with this exercise, the main objective is for you to be able to *justify* your answer.

Proud	*rude*	*complimentary*	*giving*
big-headed	*sensitive*	*harsh*	*kind*
modest	*ambitious*	*determined*	*admonishing*
ruthless	*self-obsessed*	*helpful*	*moralistic*

Look at each one as a class and see if you all agree on which characteristics belong to whom. If there is a difference of opinion, use this as a discussion opportunity to justify your answer.

Task 2: 7GD13, 8GD10, 9GD9

Use the information you have obtained from the first exercise to answer the following questions about Nigel and Edward's relationship.

- Who is the *leader*?
- Why do you think Edward goes around with Nigel?
- What do you think Nigel likes and dislikes about Edward?
- Is there any evidence that Edward *uses* Nigel for his own benefit, at this point in the play?

- Is there any evidence in this scene that Nigel allows himself to *be walked on* by Edward?

Feed back your answers to the class, and use differences of opinion as opportunities for discussion.

Task 3: 7W6, 7W14, 8W6

Imagine Edward and Nigel each have to fill in a short form for Mrs Painter, the director of the school play, telling her why they want to be in the play and what they feel they could offer. Use the information you gathered about the characters in the first two exercises to inform your writing. Bearing in mind what you already know about them, how do you think each of them would probably write about themselves? Use the format below if it helps. You could copy it into your books, before writing your answers.

Name:
Why do you want to be in this play?
What do you feel you could offer to the play?
Are there any dates or times you would not be available for rehearsal?

Focus on *Macbeth*

Task 1: 7R2, 7R18, 8R4, 9R1

Read Act One, Scene 3 of *Macbeth*.

Focusing on the characters of Macbeth and Banquo, look specifically at how each of them responds to the prophecies of the witches. Use the following questions to focus your reading.

- What is Macbeth's first response to the prophecies, which is noticed by Banquo? (line 51)
- How does Banquo feel about not being mentioned, at first, by the witches? (lines 52–61)
- What is significant about Banquo's final words to the witches at the end of this section, regarding his general response to them? (lines 60–61)
- Looking at those parts of the scene where Macbeth is speaking an *Aside*, which means he is supposedly speaking to himself, what are the different thought processes his mind goes through, as the reality of the prophecies begins to dawn on him?
- What does Banquo's warning to Macbeth (lines 120–127) tell us about his, quite different, response to the prophecies?

Feed back your answers to the class.

Task 2: 7R2, 8R4, 9R1

Using the information you gathered in the last exercise, find five words for each character that you think best sum up their response to the witches, for example: *fearful, cautious,* etc. Feed your answers back to the class.

How does this information help us to understand how they are *different* as characters, and what their characters are like? Try doing the same exercise but this time find five words which describe them as characters, for example: *ambitious, modest,* etc.

Task 3: 7W6, 7W14, 7W15, 8W13, 9W1, 9W10, 9W13

Imagine you are a casting agent trying to find suitable actors to play Macbeth and Banquo. Write a letter to an imaginary director *persuading* him or her that Nigel would make a good Banquo and Edward would make a good Macbeth. Think about the qualities that they share with the characters, and how this might help the performance of the parts. Below is an example of how the letter could start.

Dear Director,

I think I've just found our Macbeth. His name is Edward, he reminded me of Macbeth straight away. As soon as I mentioned I was a film-maker, his ambitious eyes lit up like a pin-ball machine. When he said the lines, he strode round the stage like he owned the place. Irritating as he is, I feel he seems quite apt for Macbeth.

Continue the letter and remember when writing persuasively how useful rhetorical questions, exaggeration and superlatives can be.

Drama Activities

1 Respond Now! 7D15, 7D19, 8D14, 8D15, 9D12

A good way of understanding characters is to place them in an extreme, difficult or embarrassing situation and explore what their *very first* response might be, in the first few seconds only. In groups, try putting each of the four characters we have studied in this section – Edward, Nigel, Macbeth, Banquo – into the following situations and explore their response. One or two of the group will have to act out the rest of the scenario.

- You've just been told that you have won a million pounds!
- A robber jumps out and asks for your wallet.
- A beggar asks you for food.
- You are told that you have a very smelly breath.
- You are asked whether you'd mind posing for a photograph.

Discuss how this may have helped to give you a more comprehensive understanding of the characters.

2 The Missing Scene 8D16, 9D12

After the witches vanish in Act One, Scene 3 of *Macbeth*, and the messengers arrive to fulfil the prophecy, Macbeth and Banquo continue on their journey, almost straight away. How do you think the conversation might have gone if they had had the chance to talk about the event right after the King's messengers had left? Use the information you gathered in the previous exercises to improvise the 'missing' scene.

Show each of your scenes to the group. Decide which you think is most likely and plausible, but remember not to dismiss anyone's ideas.

3 Sound Collage 7D15, 9D12

Often sounds can communicate much better than words in telling us how a person or character is feeling or what they are thinking. It is quite easy to think of sounds that reflect the main emotions.

Start by finding a sound that represents or symbolises each of the following emotions:

anger	*sadness*	*joy*	*confusion*	*shock*

Once you have looked at each group and got the hang of the idea, try relating the exercise to the story by thinking of sounds which reflect what Macbeth and Banquo are thinking or feeling at various points throughout Act One, Scene 3. They go through quite a range of feelings, especially Macbeth. See if you can represent these feelings as precisely as you can with sound. To present it, you could act out the scene and have separate people representing the sounds for a particular character.

Scene 3

Focus on the Scene

This scene introduces us to a lot of the characters who are with us for most of the play. Everyone is at the audition, battling for the limelight, eager to get what they want from the experience. Many characters in this scene have very different ideas of what will make them happy. After re-reading the scene, see if you can match up, from the list below, which characters hold which of the objectives listed opposite. Copy the list into your exercise books, and use lines to link the character to what you think they probably want during Scene 3.

Mrs Painter	I want to *be appreciated*
Alexis	I want to *be accepted*
Edward	I want to *be understood*
Gordon	I want to *be admired*
Nigel	I want to *have honour and be respected*
Timothy	I want to *do my best*
Drew	I want to *be the winner*

Share your answers with the class. Discuss differences of opinion.

Once you have decided what you think the different characters want within the scene, decide what the obstacles are that could prevent them from achieving their goal. You could start by writing their name, drawing a line towards their goal, then writing down the possible obstacles in between. For example:

Lloyd	Obstacles	Goal
	Given small part	I want to be
	Can't do voice she wants	important
	People don't take me seriously	

Feed answers back to the class.

As a writing exercise, imagine what Mrs Painter's notes might say about each of the audition candidates. We know that she is making notes throughout the scene. Re-read the scene again, if necessary, and put yourself in her shoes. What useful notes might she write next to each character? Use a box like the one below, if it helps.

Name	Comment
Edward	Super voice, a bit big-headed
Gordon	Excellent knowledge of play, good at crowd control

Make your notes extensive or brief depending on the amount of time you have.

Focus on *Macbeth*

Scene 3 is a great scene for gathering all the information you need in order to understand most of the plot from the first Act of *Macbeth*.

Begin by drawing a plot line for Act One of *Macbeth*. To show the beginning, at one end put a little arrow at the start of the line and write next to it *'Macbeth and Banquo fight on the King's behalf.'* At the other end, write, *'Macbeth and Lady Macbeth conspire to kill the King.'* Now, using the information gathered from reading Scene 3, try to fill in on the plot line all the major events which happen during the first Act. This should give you a firm understanding of how the story begins.

When Amy, Drew, Kirsty and Zara audition for the play in Scene 3, they have brought with them, ready prepared, the witches' chant from *Macbeth*, which they have imaginatively turned into a girl-band song, with an accompanying dance routine. This works very well as a song, because it is packed with a very definite rhythm, lots of rhyme and punchy alliteration. Look again at the piece they choose to sing.

> Double, double toil and trouble;
> Fire burn, and cauldron bubble.
> Fillet of a fenny snake,
> In the cauldron boil and bake;
> Eye of newt, and toe of frog,
> Wool of bat, and tongue of dog,
> Adder's fork, and blind-worm's sting,
> Lizard's leg, and howlet's wing,
> For a charm of powerful trouble,
> Like a hell-broth boil and bubble.
> Double, double toil and trouble;
> Fire burn, and cauldron bubble.

In groups, work on a reading, a performance or a song using the same piece. Be as imaginative and original as you can. Pay particular attention to how the rhythm, rhyme and alliteration help you to vocalise, and more importantly, *enjoy* the language.

Task 3: 7W3 and 6, 8W6, 9W2 and 5 and 11

As a writing exercise, write a secret diary entry for Macbeth, looking back on everything that has happened in the short time-span that Act One represents.

Imagine he is writing it right at the end of Act One. Think of all the different things that his mind has had to cope with during this short time.

Drama Activities

1 Staging the Action 7D15, 9D14

During Scene 3 Mrs Painter gives the cast an overview of all the major things that happen in Act One, by very simplistically *blocking* the important bits of action.

(Blocking is where the director tells you where to come on, where to stand, where to move to, generally any movement involved in the scene.)

This is also an excellent way for us to remember the action. Sometimes we can remember visual images better than words.

Using a small space, try to create the blocking which Mrs Painter is suggesting in the scene. She makes it quite clear where the main characters should stand and who should move where, at what point. It is not necessary for groups to say any of the actual dialogue in the scene, but it might be useful for each group, when they show the piece to the rest of the class, to say what part of the story is happening with each movement.

2 Interviewing the Characters 7D15, 8D14 and 15, 9D12

At the end of a television show, where contestants have been auditioning against each other for some prize, an interviewer will often ask them lots of questions about how they think they have done, before the winner is revealed. This is called hot-seating. You usually find contestants are either quite big-headed or quite modest in response to the questions. Some may say they thought they were much better than the others; some might just say what a tremendous experience it was, and not seem too bothered about winning.

Using volunteers to play each of the main characters in Scene 3, have the class hot-seat each one about how well they think they might have done, and what they think of the other people at the audition.

Once all the characters have been hot-seated, decide as a class which ones you think most realistically reflect each character.

Scene 4

Focus on the Scene

Looking specifically at Scene 4, discuss in small groups, *how* Alexis finally manages to persuade Edward to get rid of Mrs Painter. Who has the higher status, and is in control, within the scene?

Feed back your ideas to the class.

Put yourself in Edward's shoes during this scene. What words or phrases which Alexis uses have particular effect in persuading Edward to take the action he eventually does? Try to find five words or lines which you think have most effect on him.

Using the information you have gathered in these first two exercises, try writing a *confession* by Edward, where he admits to committing this nasty act just to serve his own ends. You could address the confession to the head teacher, or perhaps to Mrs Painter herself.

Think about how you would try and explain your actions if you were Edward. Describe how you felt when Alexis said things which really affected you. Explain how Meg's prophecy helped to fuel your idea even more. Remember to write it down in the form of a *confession*, try to sound as apologetic as you can. Use your imagination to try and put yourself in his position. Below is a possible beginning for the letter. Feel free to use this one or make up one of your own.

Dear Mrs Painter,

You may wonder why you were suddenly asked to do jury service. I am ashamed to inform you it was no accident. I can't bear this guilt any longer. It was me, Edward. It all started when . . .

To finish the exercise, volunteers could read their confession to the class, making it sound as heartfelt as possible. Decide as a class which sounded most *contrite* (this means truly sorry). If you have time, try to evaluate what it was which made these particular ones most effective.

Once you have done this, try doing the comparative tasks in the next section.

Focus on *Macbeth*

Task 1: 7R6, 8R4, 8R11, 8R16, 9R7, 9R9, 9R14

In pairs, read Act One, Scene 7 of *Macbeth*, where Macbeth and Lady Macbeth conspire to kill the King. Are there any similarities between this scene and the scene you have just looked at between Edward and Alexis? Are there any points where Lady Macbeth tries to persuade Macbeth in the same way Alexis does Edward? Try to make a list of things Lady Macbeth says which you think have an impact on Macbeth.

Feed back your ideas to the class.

Task 2: 7R14, 9WL7

In small groups, look at the context in which each of the following words or phrases are used and decide how significant they might be in persuading Macbeth towards his eventual course of action.

'drunk'	(line 35)
'green and pale'	(line 37)
'Art thou afeard'	(line 39)
'live a coward'	(line 43)
'you were a man'	(line 49)
'had I so sworn'	(line 58)

Thinking point

Do you think these words have a similar effect on Macbeth, as the words or lines you chose from Scene 3 had on Edward?

When we are given a play or any kind of story, we are never given all the information about the characters or the situation. Sometimes it is very useful to *fill in the gaps* concerning what we are not told. It helps us to understand the characters more fully, and where the play or story fits in the context of their whole lives.

Read closely what Lady Macbeth says about her husband before he arrives in Act One, Scene 5, and also how they speak to each other when he enters the scene, and later in Act One, Scene 7.

Using what you have found in the scene, in pairs try to create the history of their relationship, saying exactly when and where you think they might have met, what attracted them to each other and how they got together.

Try writing it in the form of a game show with the host introducing Macbeth and Lady Macbeth as a couple on the show. It could be scripted with each character answering different questions about their relationship, put to them by the host.

Present your ideas to the class. Make sure you *justify* the story you have given to their relationship with any clues the information in the scene gave you.

Drama Activities

1 The Power Game 7D18, 7D19, 8D15, 9D12

Look again at Scene 4 of *Macbeth on the Loose*.

This activity aims to reinforce in our minds, in a visual way, who has the power within the scene, who is in control.

In groups of four, look at the scene and decide where you think Alexis has the power and is dominating Edward, and the parts where Edward tries to regain it.

After you have done this, one pair should read the scene in front of the class, while the other pair use a single chair and stand on it whenever they think the character they are representing has the power within the scene. Most of the time it will probably be Alexis, but there are times when Edward tries to get the power back. The chair signifies a higher level, it represents who you think has the higher status within the scene.

Now, in groups, re-read Act One, Scene 7. Do the same for this scene, being very precise about *exactly* when the power shifts.

2 Forum Theatre 7D15, 7D19, 8D14, 9D12

This is a drama technique that allows members of the audience to stop the drama at any point, enter the action on stage and take over the role-play from one of the existing actors. They may decide to take the improvisation off in a completely new direction, or they may have a good idea about how a character should respond in a certain situation. Members of the audience stop the action by shouting 'Freeze', before entering the scene. It is important to be considerate of others with this exercise. Make sure before you take over from a character that they have had a reasonable attempt at the exercise.

In small groups, improvise the basic action of either scene we have looked at in this section, and use *forum theatre* to explore what other responses Edward or Macbeth *could* have had in the situation. You might start by thinking how *you* would respond in the same situation. You will not need either script for this exercise, just remember as much as you can about who is manipulating whom in the scenes, and *how* they do it.

Show your scenes to the class.

Discussion point

Think about how this exercise may have helped you to consider whether Macbeth had any real *choice* in this situation. Maybe you feel after putting yourself in the situation that many people might have responded as he did. Discuss your ideas in pairs and feed your conclusions back to the class.

Scene 5

Focus on the Scene

Task 1: 7R6, 8R4, 8R11, 9W7, 9W9, 7GD13, 9GD9

This is perhaps the first scene where we begin to see the story in *Macbeth on the Loose* mirror the story within *Macbeth*. In small groups, re-read the scene and see how many different parts you can find where the two stories cross over.

Share your ideas with the class, and add to your lists accordingly.

Task 2: 7R6, 8R4, 8R6, 9R1, 7S1, 8S1, 8S5, 7GD12, 7GD13, 8GD10, 9GD9

Use the following questions as starting points for small group discussion. Look at everything you know about the play when discussing each one. Once you have considered them, try to agree on what your answers are. Finally, feed back your conclusions to the group.

- How could this scene be said to prove Mrs Painter's earlier statement that *'things change but people don't'*?
- Do you think that the people in the play still see the story of Macbeth as old and irrelevant to them?
- One form of *dramatic irony* is where the audience or readers of the story can see the character's situation more clearly than they can. Bearing this in mind, what elements of this scene could be said to have dramatic irony?

Task 3: 7W6, 7W14, 9W1, 9W2

Notice in this scene how Mr Atherton's approach to directing *Macbeth* differs tremendously from Mrs Painter's. In pairs, discuss who you think is the better director. Explain why; list as many reasons as you can.

As a writing exercise, write an *informal* letter imagining you are Mrs Painter writing to Mr Atherton about how the play is going. What kinds of things would she be likely to ask about, with regard to the production?

Now, in groups, decide what you think Mr Atherton's response might be and formulate the reply. How would he respond to Mrs Painter's questions? Consider the information you gathered about him in the earlier part of the task to inform your response.

Focus on *Macbeth*

> ### Task 1: 7W3, 9W4, 9W12

Draw a plot line as you did for Act One, this time for Act Two. Use the information within Scene 5 to plot all the major things that happen in Act Two of *Macbeth*.

All the information you need to construct an outline for the plot of Act Two is in Scene 5. Once you have established a good understanding of the plot for this section of the story, continue with the following exercise.

> ### Task 2: 7R7, 7R12, 7R14, 8R5, 8R7, 8R10, 9R14, 9SL4

This is the first time we are properly introduced to Macduff and, as Gordon says, the most probable reason for his emergence in the scene is to accompany the King on his return journey.

Looking at the Language

Look closely at Macduff's reaction, read by Gordon, when he finds the King's dead body.

GORDON   O horror, horror, horror! Tongue nor heart
                Cannot conceive nor name thee.

EDWARD   What's the matter?

GORDON   Confusion now hath made his masterpiece.
                Most sacrilegious murder hath broke ope
                The Lord's anointed temple, and stole thence
                The life o' th' building!

EDWARD   What is't you say—the life?

KIRSTY   Mean you his Majesty?

GORDON   Approach the chamber, and destroy your sight
                With a new Gorgon. Do not bid me speak.
                See, and then speak yourselves.

Judging from this response, what kind of relationship do you think Macduff has with the King? Pick out exact phrases that you think communicate to us most effectively how he feels towards the King.

What do you think the particular relevance of the following words might be, with regard to the relationship between Macduff and the King?

> 'nor heart'
> 'Lord's anointed temple'
> 'the life'
> 'destroy your sight'

Share your ideas with the class.

Task 3: 7W3, 7W6, 8W6, 9R14, 9SL4

As you can probably see from the extracts of *Macbeth* Act Two in Scene 5 of *Macbeth on the Loose*, it is an Act that is packed with people not really saying what they are thinking. Many characters are hiding things. They are not really speaking their true thoughts.

The next exercise attempts to use *thought-tracking* as a way of getting underneath what a character says, to reveal what they are *really* thinking. Thought-tracking is a dramatic technique used to help us understand what might be going on in a character's mind where they are not speaking their true thoughts. It helps us to understand the *sub-text* of a scene. (This means what is happening beneath the lines.) The following exercise aims to thought-track certain characters at key moments throughout Act Two.

To start with, try to map the following lines onto the plot line you did earlier, roughly where you think they come in the Act. Read around each line so that you understand the context in which it is spoken.

> Act Two, Scene 2, line 21
>
> Macbeth (to Lady Macbeth) *This is a sorry sight.*
>
> Act Two, Scene 3, line 100
>
> Macduff (to Macbeth) *Wherefore did you so?*
>
> Act Two, Scene 3, line 111
>
> Lady Macbeth (to all) *Help me hence, ho!*
>
> Act Two, Scene 3, line 128
>
> Malcolm (to Donalbain) *What will you do? Let's not consort with them.*
>
> Act Two, Scene 4, line 37
>
> Macduff (to Ross) *Well may you see things well done there:- adieu Lest our old robes sit easier than our new.*

Once you have understood what is meant by each of the quotations, try writing, in just a couple of lines, what the characters might *truly* be thinking, at the time when they speak each of them. For example the first one might be something like:

'I can't believe what I've done! I should never have let her talk me into this.'

Share your ideas with the class. See if you all agree on what the characters would be thinking.

Drama Activities

1 Hot-Seating the Characters 7D15, 8D14, 9D12

Act Two, Scene 3 has so many characters *thinking* different things, *pretending* different things and holding different *hidden agendas*, that it makes an excellent scene with which to use the dramatic technique of *hot-seating,* as a means of really getting to the bottom of what is going on.

Hot-seating, as we saw in the activities for the previous scene, is where the character has to sit in front of an audience while they ask him or her questions about different aspects of the situation they are in. The audience can be as direct and personal with the questions as they wish. The character can get as heated as they wish, in response. That is why the seat gets hot!

Try putting different volunteers into the hot-seat. You could either have a few people hot-seated as the same character (this is especially useful where there is a difference of opinion about how that character might respond) or else hot-seat each of the main characters just once.

---

2 Putting Yourself in Mr Atherton's Shoes 7D15, 8D14, 8D16, 9D13, 9D15

This exercise aims to develop and assess how thorough your understanding is of various parts in Act Two, Scene 3. It asks you to *direct* different sections as you think they ought to be done, bearing in mind what you know of the situation and what each character is thinking and feeling. The direction you give to others about how each character should move, speak or gesture is your own *interpretation* of the text.

Looking at Scene 5, you can see Mr Atherton does not really seem to have any idea of how this Act should be directed. He cannot give Lloyd any help with Fleance's character. He fails to understand the importance of the dagger scene and wants to skip over it. Gordon has to explain to him why Lady Macbeth smears the hands of the King's servants with blood. He has to ask Gordon why Macduff is there, and finally has to ask everyone how the Act ends.

In small groups with enough people so that each is a character in the scene, put yourself into Mr Atherton's shoes and take it in turns to direct short sections of Act Two, Scene 3, from where Macduff arrives at the castle. Use the extracts from *Macbeth on the Loose* Scene 5 if you wish, or if you prefer, direct a different section from the original *Macbeth* text. Use what the characters say about this part of the story in Scene 5 to help your understanding. Also consider the following points when directing your actors.

- the way the characters move around
- physical gestures they might use
- the way they speak the lines
- what they are feeling or thinking at given points.

The thought-tracking and hot-seating exercises you did earlier should really help with this exercise. Use as much as you can of what you discovered about the characters and the situation.

Scene 6

Focus on the Scene

Once you have read this scene, compare and contrast it with Scene 4, the earlier scene between Alexis and Edward in the park. Discuss, from the information within each scene, how each of the characters has changed. List the changes, if it is easier.

Feed back your ideas to the class.

Now look at what has happened in between the scenes and discuss what events could have happened which might have contributed to these changes.

Imagine Alexis keeps a diary, like many people do, which records what has happened in her day, and her personal reflections on the events. As a writing exercise, write two diary entries.

- Make the first one on the day of Scene 4, in which she and Edward are in the park for the first time. What comments might she have made about her new boyfriend, bearing in mind what happens in Scene 4?

- Make the second entry on the day that Scene 6 takes place. As she details what they spoke of in the park, how might she describe the recent changes in Edward? How does she feel about the person whom he seems to be becoming?

If you have time, share your entries with the class. See if there is a general agreement about what she might write.

Think now about how Edward might feel about his own actions here. Does he actually *enjoy* plotting and scheming other people's downfall? What is at stake for Edward here, if he doesn't get Nigel out of the way?

As a short writing exercise, consider the following. If Edward was to write a *pros and cons* list about each course of action (a list which has the advantages on one side (*pros*) and the disadvantages on the other (*cons*)) what might each list look like? Think first about the *pros* of *getting* rid of him, then the list for *cons*. Set it out as below, copying the table into your books.

Pros of getting rid of Nigel	Cons
Can't tell on me if he ain't there	He'll never be my mate again

Focus on *Macbeth*

Task 1: 7R6, 8R11, 9R7, 9R9, 7GD13, 8GD10, 9GD9

Read Act Three, Scene 2 of *Macbeth*.

In small groups, compare and contrast this scene with Scene 6 of *Macbeth on the Loose*. Discuss how Edward's situation is similar to Macbeth's. What are the similarities?

Think also about Lady Macbeth. How is her response to Macbeth – in Act Three, Scene 2 – similar to Alexis's response to Edward in Scene 6?

To help focus your reading, consider the following questions.

- What feelings do Macbeth and Edward share in these two contrasting scenes?
- What are they both thinking about?
- Do Lady Macbeth and Alexis share the burden of anxiety expressed by both their partners?

Task 2: 7S2, 8S2

As a speaking and listening exercise, in pairs, imagine you are one of Lady Macbeth's servants, who happened to overhear the discussion between Lady Macbeth and her husband in Act Three, Scene 2.

Overwhelmed by the scandalous content of their discussion, you rush to recount the story to a friend. How might you retell the story? What kind of language would you use?

Each have a go, and be aware of how *your* version differs from the *written* story.

Feed back your observations to the class.

Task 3: 7R2, 8R4, 9R1, 8W8, 9W1, 9W11

The following exercise aims to develop your ability to *summarise* when reading and to extract from the text only the *essential* information.

Look again at Act Three, Scene 2, and focus on how Shakespeare uses tremendous imagery to expand as much as he can on how Macbeth is feeling at this point. How might you condense each of the speeches Macbeth has in this scene into one or two lines of contemporary English?

In pairs, try rewriting the scene in your own version. Be as original as you can when considering what language to use when changing it to modern-day speech.

Drama Activities

1 Taking Edward to Court! 7D15, 8D15, 8D16, 9D12

This exercise aims to test your understanding of what the different pressures are upon our protagonist in the drama, Edward – afterwards you could do the same exercise with Macbeth, if you wish.

Imagine Edward has been taken to court, found guilty of conspiracy to get rid of Nigel, and has pleaded guilty.

In groups, one person act as Edward, one, the prosecutor, one as Edward's defence lawyer and one as the judge. What are the arguments that you could put forward for either a harsh sentence, if you are the prosecutor, or a lenient one, if you are the defence lawyer?

If you are the judge, think about each of the views carefully. Once you have made your final decision, be clear, when delivering your verdict, what exactly swayed you towards one decision or another.

If you are playing Edward, think about how you might respond to the prosecutor's harsh line of questioning. How might you plead your case best?

Once you have rehearsed your piece a few times, present it to the class. Discuss and evaluate which parts of each scene were most persuasive.

Scene 7

Focus on the Scene

In this scene the story parallels the story of *Macbeth* at the same time, and in quite a lot of different ways. The cast are rehearsing Act Three, Scene 4 of *Macbeth*. Look at the different parts of the scene they are doing and see if you can find the elements which happen in the scene, but which also happen in their story. To help you, below are some parts of their story which have parallels in *Macbeth*.

Their story	Macbeth
Edward sees Nigel.	
Edward is made to feel guilty by Nigel's presence because he knows he was the one who got rid of him.	
Nigel stares at Edward, trying to haunt him.	
Edward can't contain his guilt any more and shouts at Nigel.	
Alexis tries to make excuses for his behaviour, so the others don't suspect anything.	
The cast don't understand Edward's outburst.	

Share your answers with the class.

As a writing exercise, imagine Mr Atherton is very concerned about the strange behaviour that Edward was manifesting at the rehearsal, and has communicated the details to a medical professional.

The doctor has asked one or two members of the cast to write a short *report* outlining what happened and has given them the sheet below to fill in. Decide what character you are and try filling in the sheet. Copy the table into your books, leaving as much space as you think you need for each section.

Name of witness:
Time of incident:
Date of incident:
Describe how the incident occurred:
Any other relevant details:

Remember with report writing to keep the tone *factual*. Avoid any reference to how you felt, and don't make any speculations about what it could all have been about. Make the focus purely what you saw and heard.

Task 3: 8R7, 7GD12, 8GD10, 9GD9

Discuss, in groups, how the writer makes use of *irony* in this scene. Remember – irony means that the audience or readers of the drama can see characters' situations more profoundly than the characters can.

Think about the following questions in your discussion.

- How does this irony add humour to the scene?
- How does it engage the reader or watcher?
- How could it help to communicate meaning?

Feed back your ideas to the class. See if there is an agreement about how irony is used. Where there are differences of opinion, use these occasions as opportunities for developing a reasoned discussion.

Focus on *Macbeth*

Look again at the section of text Alexis and Edward read in Scene 7 (from *Macbeth* Act Three, Scene 4), in which Macbeth is supposed to have seen Banquo's ghost. Look again at his outburst against the vision and how Alexis, as Lady Macbeth, tries to persuade the dinner guests that Macbeth's behaviour is nothing to be concerned about. Here it is again below.

KIRSTY	Here is a place reserved, sir.
EDWARD	Where?

Kirsty points to an empty chair.

KIRSTY	Here my good lord.

Edward, as Macbeth, hadn't seen the empty seat, because Banquo's ghost occupies it. He notices who it is.

KIRSTY	What is't that moves your Highness?
MR ATHERTON	Now, Macbeth, this is where you see the ghost.
EDWARD	Which of you have done this?
LORDS	What, my good lord?
EDWARD	(*to the ghost*) Thou canst not say I did it; never shake Thy gory locks at me.
SCOTT	Gentlemen, rise, his Highness is not well.

During Alexis's next section, Edward keeps glancing round and becomes increasingly uncomfortable with Nigel's presence.

ALEXIS	Sit, worthy friends. My lord is often thus, And hath been from his youth. Pray you keep seat, The fit is momentary, upon a thought He will again be well. If much you note him, You shall offend him, and extend his passion. Feed, and regard him not.

Discuss the following questions in pairs.

- Do you think Macbeth realises that he is the only one who can see the vision?
- Why do you think he talks to the ghost? What is he trying to achieve when he first addresses him?
- How persuasive is Lady Macbeth's explanation, which Alexis reads?
- If you were a dinner guest at the party, would you accept her explanation and be able to continue with your dinner?
- To what other things might the dinner guests attribute his behaviour?

Look now, in the original *Macbeth* text, at how the scene progresses. Does the situation resolve here or get worse?

Task 2: 7W6, 9W2, 9W5

The following exercise develops your ability to write *from different perspectives* and tests your knowledge of the action within the scene.

Imagine you are a guest at the dinner party Macbeth is holding. When you return home from the party, you write an account in your diary of what it was like. How do you think a guest might account for the action of the evening? Detail your thoughts, as the character, in the diary extract. Remember to see the action from the perspective of a dinner guest. Think about how much less they would understand about the situation than we do.

Task 3: 7S1, 8S5, 7GD12, 8GD10, 9GD9

In small groups, discuss which aspects of this scene help to create an overall feeling of *tension*. Once you have brainstormed ideas, try to list the different elements that contribute to it. Consider the following things and allow them to inform your discussion:

- the atmosphere at the beginning of the scene
- what the guests hear Macbeth say to the ghost
- the relationship Lady Macbeth is trying to maintain with her guests, despite Macbeth's behaviour

- the fact that only Macbeth can see the ghost.

Once you have discussed your ideas, feed back your conclusions to the class.

Drama Activities

1 Thought-Tracking the Characters 7D15, 7D19, 8D15, 8D16, 9D12

Because this scene is so full of sub-text – remember, this is what characters are thinking and feeling, but not saying – it makes a very good scene with which to use thought-tracking to get to the bottom of what is really going on.

Try re-enacting the basic action of Act Three, Scene 4 of *Macbeth*, just from your memory, and thought-track the characters at the following times:

- Macbeth, when he sees the ghost
- Lady Macbeth, when Macbeth shouts at the vision
- the guests, when Macbeth shouts at the vision
- Lady Macbeth, after she's given her initial explanation of Macbeth's behaviour to the guests
- the guests, after they have listened to Lady Macbeth's explanation.

Present each of your scenes to the class. Which part of each one do you think truly reflects what they would be thinking?

Extend the exercise to include other parts of the scene that would be good moments at which to thought-track the characters.

2 Conscience Alley 7D18, 8D15, 9D12

This is a group exercise that gives everyone a chance to contribute in building a collage of accusing thoughts which a character might experience, if they know they have acted wrongly, and are prisoners of their own conscience.

The class form two lines facing each other so that there is a tunnel between them for someone to walk through. Choose a character who you think is experiencing a bad conscience and have them slowly walk through the tunnel, between the two lines, with their eyes closed. As they pass each person, those people quietly whisper one thought they think the character is trying to suppress, about what they have done. For example, if the character doing the exercise was Macbeth, one whispered thought might be, *'He was your friend'*.

Try the exercise with Macbeth and Lady Macbeth. How are their consciences different?

Try repeating the whispered thoughts, letting them build, one on top of another, until the very last has been spoken. If you are the person walking the tunnel, as the character, think about how these whispers make you feel inside. How do they make you want to respond?

Scene 8

Focus on the Scene

> ### Task 1: 7R6, 7R7, 7R8, 7R15, 8R4, 8R5, 8R10, 9R1

From looking at what Alexis says during this scene, what do you think has happened to her since Scene 4 of the play, in which she was encouraging Edward to be more ruthless? What are the things that might have contributed to her becoming more compassionate about others in this scene?

Compare and contrast both characters in this scene with how they acted earlier in Scene 4. Try to spot as many differences as you can between what they were and what they are now.

Share your ideas with the class.

> ### Task 2: 7W7, 9W5

The writer in this scene tries to make the reader or watcher of the drama *curious* about what the characters are doing at the start of the scene, by *withholding information* about why they are ticking names off a list. This is quite a common device writers use, and it's a good way of keeping the audience's interest: they keep watching or reading in order to find out the information that is being withheld. See if you can find the line in the scene where it first becomes clear what they are up to.

As a writing exercise, create an alternative beginning to this scene, which uses this same technique of *withholding information* to keep the reader's attention. You could have the characters talking about the problem of what to do about the ginger-haired males, without actually mentioning ginger hair. You could talk around the subject without ever actually being too specific. Try a few ideas out in pairs, or groups, and see which one works best.

Once you have written your new beginnings, read them to the class. Decide which you think is best and why.

It seems, from looking at this scene, that Alexis is not enjoying something which, if you remember, *she started*.

Can you empathise with her situation? (This means 'understand and sympathise with her'.) Have you ever wanted something to happen an awful lot, then when it does, realised it's not what you thought it would be, and ended up trying to get out of the situation?

If you have, share your stories with the class.

Focus on *Macbeth*

Task 1: 7R6, 7R7, 7R8, 8R4, 8R5, 8R7, 9R1, 7GD13, 8GD10, 9GD9

Read Act Five, Scene 1 of *Macbeth*.

Here we see Lady Macbeth sleepwalking and talking about the cruel actions she and Macbeth have perpetrated. What do you think the blood represents, that she can't wash away? If it *symbolised* something else, what would it be?

Does Lady Macbeth share the same kinds of feelings that Alexis is experiencing in this scene? What are the feelings that they might share? Discuss in small groups and feed back your conclusions to the class.

Task 2: 7R6, 8R4, 9R1

We know that in Scene 7 of *Macbeth on the Loose*, Edward is given a warning by Meg, the tea lady, about a male with ginger hair who could spoil his plan to play Macbeth and become a star. This is what drives him to start calculating how to dispose of ginger-haired males in this present scene.

Read Act Four, Scene 1 of *Macbeth*.

Here we see Macbeth visit the witches a second time, to find out more about the predictions they made concerning him. What do they warn him about, after they've given him the predictions he sought?

Bearing in mind what Edward's response was to the tea lady's warning, in small groups decide how you think Macbeth will respond to *his* warning. Try to predict what is going to happen in the story. Once you have made your prediction, read ahead, in the original text, and see if you were right.

Task 3: 7S1, 7S2, 8S2, 9S1, 7GD13, 8GD10, 9GD9

As a speaking and listening exercise, discuss, in groups, what you think it is which drives people like Edward and Macbeth into seeking power and prestige at the cost of everything else. Have you ever wanted something so much that you were prepared to sacrifice other things to get it?

Share your thoughts and personal experiences with the group.

Testing Your Scruples!

Now put yourself in Edward's shoes. Imagine that you are promised the same things Edward is assured of by Meg, 'Television parts. Film offers. Celebrity parties!' If all this was promised to you, what would *you* sacrifice in order to get it? Friends? Honesty?

If you dare, share the depths that you think you could stoop to in order to get your prize.

Drama Activities

1 Edward's Dream 7D15, 8D16, 9D12

What is it about Meg's prediction for Edward that fills his head with so many desirable ideas, and drives him to be so calculating in order to achieve them? What are the parts of the dream which give him most pleasure?

In groups, work on an *improvisation* which depicts Edward's perfect world, once his dream has been realised. Perhaps it's a scene with fans throwing themselves at him, or being surrounded by beautiful females. What do you think he wants most? Try to encapsulate your essential ideas into five freeze-frames, which come to life for a few seconds each. Each one can depict a different aspect of the dream.

Present your ideas to the class. See if you can agree on which one suits Edward's character most.

2 Alexis's Nightmare 7D15, 8D16, 9D12

Contrast this first exercise with an improvisation depicting what Alexis is *frightened* will happen, if Edward remains on his present course of action.

Look again at Scene 8 and decide what you think she is most *scared* of as the scene ends. Whom is she frightened for, herself or Edward? What is the worst that could happen, if her fears come true? Use freeze-frames again, this time to depict the worst that could happen, as Edward's obsession with the prediction gets worse. As before, allow each frame to come to life for just a few seconds each.

Once you have done both of the above exercises, you could try presenting them together. Often placing two contrasting scenes together like this can be quite effective in helping us to understand the action more fully. We call this *juxtaposing* scenes.

Scene 9

Focus on the Scene

Task 1: 7R6, 8R4, 7S1, 8S1

Discuss what Gordon and Timothy are like as characters. What characteristics do they demonstrate in this scene? How are they different as characters? See if you can find three words to describe each of them.

Share your ideas with the class, then try the comparative exercise in Task 1 of the next section.

Task 2: 7R2, 7R7, 8R4, 9R1

This exercise aims to develop your ability to *summarise* (your ability to condense long sections of text, or action, into the key moments which give *continuity* to the story).

Imagine you are Gordon, at the end of this scene, writing an email to a friend about everything that has happened since he began doing it. Try to include all the events, or things that happened, which give *continuity* to the story.

Once you have done this, read your pieces to the class. If others mention key things you have missed, which you feel are important to understanding the story as a whole, redraft your email message accordingly.

Task 3: 7S1, 8S1, 7W3, 9W4

In the second half of this scene, Edward returns to the rehearsal with enormous energy and confidence. He is convinced nothing can stop him from becoming *King* of the play. He does not even seem to care that Alexis has now left the play because of his behaviour. How has Edward changed from the person he was at the beginning of the play? Discuss.

See if you can map the journey his character has made. Draw a line similar to the plot line, and at one end put *'Edward auditions with Nigel'*. At the other end put *'Edward has become merciless'*. Try to plot on the line all the things that have happened that may have contributed to the change in his character.

Once you have done this, try doing the comparative exercise in Task 3 of the next section.

Focus on *Macbeth*

Task 1: 7R6, 8R4, 8R5, 9R7, 9R9

Read Act Four, Scene 3 of *Macbeth*.

Do you think Gordon shares any qualities with the character he is playing? What are they? What about Timothy? Is he similar to the character of Malcolm?

In some ways Act Four, Scene 3 of *Macbeth* and Scene 9 of *Macbeth on the Loose* are quite similar, but there are also a few differences. What do you think they are? In Scene 8 of *Macbeth on the Loose*, Timothy really doesn't believe, to start with, that he would be good playing Macbeth, in a sense being *King* of the play. Does Malcolm honestly think during Act Four, Scene 3 of *Macbeth* that he would not be a good king? In pairs, read the scene in detail and discuss your ideas. If you have time, feed your conclusions back to the class.

Task 2: 7W6, 7R14, 8R7, 8W7, 9WL7, 9R14, 9SL4

Look again at the speech Edward makes as Macbeth. Here it is again, below.

EDWARD   Bring me no more reports, let them fly all.
Till Birnam wood remove to Dunsinane
I cannot taint with fear. What's the boy Malcolm?
Was he not born of woman? The spirits that know
All mortal consequences have pronounced me thus:
'Fear not, Macbeth: no man that's born of woman
Shall e'er have power upon thee.' Then fly, false thanes,
And mingle with the English epicures.
The mind I sway by, and the heart I bear,
Shall never sag with doubt, nor shake with fear.

Enter Lara as servant.

The devil damn thee black, thou cream-faced loon!
Where gott'st thou that goose look?

LARA   There is ten thousand—

EDWARD   Geese, villain?

LARA   Soldiers sir.

EDWARD   Go prick thy face, and over-red thy fear,
Thou lily-livered boy. What soldiers, patch?
Death of thy soul, those linen cheeks of thine
Are counsellors to fear. What soldiers, whey-face?

Lara mimes looking from the window.

LARA   The English force, so please you.

EDWARD   Take thy face hence.

The *tone* of Edward's speech is extremely *arrogant* (which means proud and overbearing). Discuss what has given Macbeth this arrogance. The clues are in the text itself.

In pairs, try drawing out the words that you think gives the speech this kind of *tone*.

Why are these words particularly effective? What *associations* do they have which make them either conceited, or else derogatory to the servant?

As a writing exercise, try changing the *tone* of the speech, by rewriting it and replacing the words which make it arrogant with words that make it more *modest* (which means not so big-headed). For example, instead of starting it, *'Bring me no more reports, let them fly all'*, you could begin, *'Don't worry about bringing me any more reports, I'm not too concerned about what they say.'*

Changing the tone of writing is quite fun and it helps you to understand how to write for different purposes and contexts. Once you have finished the exercise, read your speeches to the class. Decide which you think have transformed the speech best.

Macbeth feels himself to be invincible at this point, whereas at the start of the play he was much less confident. Try doing the same exercise with Macbeth that you did with Edward in Task 3 of the last section. Try to map the journey his character has made and the things that have contributed to the change.

Draw a line similar to the plot line and, at one end, put '*Macbeth fights nobly on the King's behalf*' and at the other, '*Macbeth feels he is invincible in the fight for his own glory*'. Use the information in the scenes you have read so far to plot his journey.

Share your ideas with the class and if necessary adjust your ideas accordingly.

Drama Activities

1 Make the Emotion Physical! 7D15, 7D18, 8D15, 8D16, 9D12

This doesn't mean punch someone if you feel angry! This exercise is about *representing* a feeling or an emotion with a *physical position*. It can help us a great deal in identifying with a character and understanding the different emotions present in a single moment of action.

Scene 9 is quite a long scene and different characters go through a lot of different emotions and feelings. In small groups, each represent a character from Scene 9. See if, with each character, you can find five different emotions that they feel at some point during the scene.

For example, if you were representing Timothy, you might start feeling *scared* by Gordon's entrance, then *angry,* when Gordon tells you what Edward has done, then perhaps *despondent*, when you feel you couldn't play Macbeth anyway.

Find an *exaggerated physical position* to represent each emotion you feel as that character.

Present each group to the class. Show each character's progression of emotion, in turn. One of the group could clap to end one position and start another.

2 Putting the Characters Together 7D15, 7D18, 8D15, 8D16, 9D12

Try using what you have just done in the previous task to put the characters together to see what they are feeling at the *same* moment of action. Use the same kind of physical positioning to represent their feelings at the following points:

- Gordon bursts in
- Timothy reads the note
- Timothy reads the scene well
- the rest of the cast enter
- Edward realises he dies at the end of the play
- Edward reveals Alexis has left the play
- Gordon grabs Charlie's note to Edward.

Once you have presented each of the pieces to the class, you could try doing the same for either Act Four, Scene 3 or Act Five, Scene 3.

Scene 10

Focus on the Scene

Scene 10 is a very short scene but it fulfils a very practical function within the play. It gives us, as the reader or watcher of the drama, some necessary *exposition* with regard to the story. This word means *an explanation*, things that we would have to understand in order to follow the rest of the story.

Re-read the scene and focus on the information it gives us that we would *have to* receive in order to understand the rest of the play.

Share your findings with the class.

In small groups, discuss what the tea ladies give to the story in *Macbeth on the Loose*. Brainstorm the following questions.

- Do they have important *functions* in the play?
- If they do, what do you think they are?
- Do you think they add *humour* to the story? If so, how?
- Do you think they add *irony* to the story? If so, how?

Imagine that your teacher wants to perform *Macbeth on the Loose*, but needs to cut certain scenes to reduce the performance time. He or she suggests that perhaps the tea ladies' scenes could be cut. How would your group respond to that suggestion?

As a writing exercise, write a letter to the teacher either agreeing or disagreeing with their suggestion. Use bullet points, listing reasons why either the scenes can, or can't, be cut.

Share your letters with the class.

As a speaking and listening exercise, hold a *debate* as to whether you think the tea ladies are wholly or partly responsible for Edward's downfall. You could divide the class into large groups, with two opposing teams, and debate the issue, using all the information you have from the text.

You could extend the debate by asking whether *anyone* nowadays should believe or be swayed by things like horoscopes, clairvoyants, or crystal balls. What sort of responsibility do the people behind these things have, when they guide people in the decisions they make?

Once you have done this, try the comparative exercises in the next section.

Focus on *Macbeth*

Task 1: 7R6, 8R4, 7S1, 8S5

Re-read Act One, Scenes 1 and 3, and Act Four, Scene 1 of *Macbeth*.

Use this information to look at the following questions, in pairs.

- What function do the witches have in *Macbeth*?
- What are the main differences between the witches and the tea ladies?
- What motive do they have, when pursuing their evil activities?
- Why do they choose Macbeth to heap misfortune on?

Feed back your ideas to the class.

Task 2: 7S1, 8S5

Decide in groups whether you think Macbeth is responsible for his own downfall, or whether the witches are wholly or partly responsible. Is Edward's case any different from Macbeth's? Use the information you gathered in the last section to help you here.

Share your ideas with the class and where there is a difference of opinion, use this as an opportunity for discussion or debate.

Task 3: 7W15, 8W8, 8W13, 9W1, 9W12, 9W13

Imagine you are one of the witches from *Macbeth*, who has been found guilty of witchcraft and of giving Macbeth prophecies which have eventually led to the murder of several people.

When brought before a judge to plead that he be lenient with her and not sentence her to death, how could she blame Macbeth for what happened after the prophecies were given to him?

As a writing exercise, in pairs, try *scripting the scene* of the witch before the judge. Consider what her different arguments might be, when attempting to defend her actions. You could start the scene as below.

JUDGE	You are accused of witchcraft and of murder. How do you plead?
WITCH	Not guilty, your honour. It's his fault!
JUDGE	Why?
WITCH	Because ...

Continue the scene. Remember to include any dialogue the judge might speak as the witch is giving her defence.

Once you have done the scene you could take turns in performing it to the class. See which ones come up with the most convincing argument. Which, if any, made you feel sorry for the witch?

Drama Activities

1 Hot-Seating 7D15, 7D17, 8D14, 8D15, 8D16, 9D12

Use this drama activity to change the emphasis from the last two sections, and put Edward and Macbeth on the spot, with responsibility for what happens after the prophecies are given. Decide in groups what arguments make *them* the guilty parties, rather than the tea ladies or the witches.

Allow two or three people to be hot-seated as each character. Which arguments were most convincing?

2 Multiple Hot-Seats 7D15, 7D17, 8D14, 8D15, 8D16, 9D12

You could try including in the hot-seat, together with Edward or Macbeth, the tea ladies or the witches. Hot-seat them all together, allow them to point and blame each other. You could almost make it like *The Jerry Springer Show!* *with today as our guests, Macbeth and the Witches!*

Others in the group could act as Jerry Springer himself, or maybe even security, if things get too heated.

Scene 11

Focus on the Scene

Task 1: 7S1, 8S1, 8S5, 9S1

The last part of the play deals with how Edward's plan is finally thwarted. After reading Scene 11, discuss what it is which finally shatters his confidence. Why does he respond the way he does when Gordon reveals his ginger hair? What was all his confidence based on? Discuss.

Once you have done this, try the comparative exercise in Task 1 of the next section.

Task 2: 9W5

As Scene 11 is the final scene in the play, discuss as a group whether you like this ending. Does it tie the story up well? What *are* the final strands that are tied up in this last scene? Is there anything that is left unresolved? Is it satisfying as an ending? Were you hoping for or expecting something else to happen? What else *could* have happened?

As a writing exercise, in pairs, devise an *alternative ending*. You could either devise a whole new final scene, or if you'd prefer, you could keep some of the existing one, and alter it in as many ways as you can. Remember though, you must make sure you tie up loose ends and not leave the reader thinking, *'What about so and so, what happened to him?'*

Once you have written your pieces you could share them with the class. Discuss which ones you think are most credible.

Task 3: 7W19, 8W18, 9W16

What are your personal feelings about *Macbeth on the Loose*, now that you have looked at it and studied it in its entirety? Did you enjoy it? Would you recommend it to anyone? Has it been useful? If so, how? What are its good and bad points?

As a final writing exercise on the play, imagine you have been asked to write a review of it for the school magazine. What aspects of the play are things that you feel you would definitely want to include writing about, in the review? You could comment on how it relates to the original text of *Macbeth*, its humour, characters that you either liked or didn't like, parts that you thought were effective, or not so effective. Include anything you think a potential reader might want to know.

Focus on *Macbeth*

Task 1: 7S1, 8S1, 8S5, 9S1, 9S9

At the exact moment that Gordon rips off his helmet and Edward flounders, Macbeth's confidence also begins to go. Discuss what it is that Gordon says, as Macduff, at the same time as he shows his ginger hair, which might affect Macbeth's confidence also. You may have to re-read sections of Scene 8 to fully understand why.

Task 2: 7W8, 8W6, 9W6

In the final scene Mr Atherton is having terrible problems trying to get exactly the right atmosphere for the beginning of the big scene, where Macduff finally meets Macbeth on the plain.

Look at what his suggestions are, with regard to lighting and sound, and the way he has positioned the characters on the stage. Can you see the effect he is trying to achieve? Look at the bits of original *Macbeth* text in the scene. What kind of atmosphere do *you* think this scene ought to have?

Bearing in mind what you know about this final scene, either from Scene 11 of *Macbeth on the Loose*, or from your reading of the original *Macbeth* text, decide on how you would build the right atmosphere for it. Think about how you would position the characters and use different levels throughout the scene to show status. Also, consider how you might use lighting, sound and set construction to stage the scene in exactly the right way.

Use the story-board technique to illustrate your ideas. Divide a page into six boxes and use each box to represent each important moment, as the scene progresses. Use captions to indicate where there is a change of lighting or where a sound effect is introduced. Discuss what different colours and sounds make you think of, when considering your lighting and sound ideas.

Task 3: 7S1, 8S1, 8S5, 9S1, 9S9

By this time you should have a fairly good understanding of what happens in the story of *Macbeth*, and what you think it could be about. Discuss the following questions, in groups.

- What is the message behind the story of *Macbeth*?
- If you had to say *Macbeth* was about two things, what would they be?
- Do you think its message still has relevance today?
- Where do you see people like Macbeth in today's society?

Once you have discussed the questions in small groups, feed your answers back to the class. Allow it to develop into a whole-class discussion.

Drama Activities

1 Pitching your Idea 7D16, 9D14

A common way for directors to enthuse their cast about how a scene might look or feel, is by *pitching* them their idea or vision for the scene. To *pitch* an idea means to explain what happens during each part of the action, making it as dramatic as possible. By doing this, the actors can understand what kind of atmosphere the director is trying to achieve, and it might also help them play their role for that particular part.

Imagine you and your team have to enthuse the rest of the class about your idea for the staging of the scene between Macduff and Macbeth. Think about how you could present your idea to the class, making it as dramatic as possible. Perhaps certain people in your group could vocalise the sound effects, others might represent where the actors would stand and how they would look. Most important of all, you need a *narrator* who tells the class what is happening at each moment. For example it might start with the narrator saying in a dramatic voice,

The scene opens in darkness with just the sound of distant rumbles of thunder. Suddenly a flash of lightning gives us a glimpse of a silhouette, a man on a hill in the distance, while Macbeth is at the forefront of the stage with his back to the man.

With this idea, two of the group would represent the characters, standing in the appropriate places, another member of the group could vocalise the sound effects of the thunder and lightning, while the other narrates the action.

Once you have practised the scene, present each version to the class. Try to agree on which one is most appropriate for the final scene. Make sure each group justifies their ideas as much as they can.

2 Macbeth *Reduced!* 7D16, 7D19

As a final exercise, you need to combine your knowledge of the basic plot of *Macbeth* with your understanding of how each piece of action follows on from the last.

Try *condensing* each important part of the story into just a few lines of dialogue, spoken by the characters. You don't have to repeat any exact lines from the text, just get the gist of what they are saying, and put it into your own words. Then put all of these together, making the whole story not more than two minutes.

Once you have worked on the pieces, present them to the class. Afterwards, award points for the quickest, but also deduct points if you feel a group has missed out important points in the story.